Dream SEWING SPACES

DESIGN & ORGANIZATION FOR SPACES LARGE & SMALL

Lynette Ranney Black

Edited by Pati Palmer
Designed by Linda Wisner
Illustrated by Jeannette Schilling & Kate Pryka

A PALMER/PLETSCH PUBLICATION

This book is dedicated to my wonderful family: my husband, Paul, who can take my ideas formulated in my head and barely sketched out on paper and miraculously make them work and look great; my daughters, Kelsey and Jessi, who tried to be patient with my work hours and to not ask too many times, "Mommy, when are we going to be a family again?"; and to my sister, Kelley, who compassionately listened to my whims and woes.

Many thanks to a friend who is always there when you need her, author and sewing expert Gail Brown, who happily lent her collection of sewing antiques that grace the pages of this book.

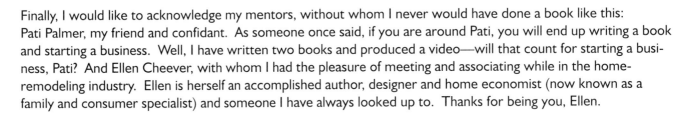

Special thanks to the multi-talented Linda Wisner and Jeannette Schilling who spent hours making my awful drawings look great! And special thanks to Ann Price Gosch, the wonderful editor who smooths my prose and catches my grammatical slips.

Thanks to John Rizzo and his assistant, Michael, for the beautiful room photography that appears throughout the book, and to Pati Palmer and Jeannette Schilling for the close-ups of the beautiful antiques. Thanks bunches to Mary Mulari and Debra Justice who saved me a bundle by providing their own photography of their lovely sewing spaces. Also, thanks to Pati Palmer, Marta Alto, Linda Wisner, Barbara Weiland, Joanne DiBenedetto and Jo Reimer for allowing their spaces to be photographed and shared with all who see this book. Special kudos to Jo for adding additional ideas to be included in the book and coming up with the word "lagniappe." Thanks to Kathleen Spike, Catherine Stephenson and Paula Marineau for sharing sections of their space with us.

Finally, I would like to acknowledge my mentors, without whom I never would have done a book like this: Pati Palmer, my friend and confidant. As someone once said, if you are around Pati, you will end up writing a book and starting a business. Well, I have written two books and produced a video—will that count for starting a business, Pati? And Ellen Cheever, with whom I had the pleasure of meeting and associating while in the home-remodeling industry. Ellen is herself an accomplished author, designer and home economist (now known as a family and consumer specialist) and someone I have always looked up to. Thanks for being you, Ellen.

Whenever brand names are mentioned, it is only to indicate to the consumer products which we have personally tested and with which we have been pleased. It is also meant to save our students time. There may be other products that are comparable to aid you in your sewing.

Copyright © 1996 by Palmer/Pletsch Incorporated.
Library of Congress Catalog Card Number: 95-72992
Published by Palmer/Pletsch Publishing, P.O. Box 12046, Portland, OR 97212-0046. U.S.A.
Printed by Craftsman Press, Seattle, WA, U.S.A. Separations and film work by Wy'East, Portland, OR.

ISBN 0-935278-41-9

TABLE OF CONTENTS

FOREWORD BY PATI PALMER

Sewing items and storage containers can fit into any part of your home, revealing a little about your personality, and making your sewing life easier! The photos below are taken from the rooms shown through out this book. These ideas and many more can be found by looking carefully at all the nooks and crannies revealed in each photograph.

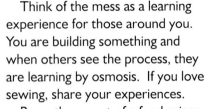

This is the most complete book ever written about sewing spaces. Lynette Ranney Black has a unique background that combines experience in the industries of sewing, kitchen and bath design, and remodeling.

Remember that sewing is an art, not a science. You need a space to help you be as creative as possible. You need it to be available at all times. Ideally, your sewing machine should never be "put away." If a food processor and toaster can decorate your kitchen counters, why can't a sewing machine be out and functional as well? Is the mess we make when cooking any different from the mess we make while sewing? So why do people worry more about their sewing messes?

Think of the mess as a learning experience for those around you. You are building something and when others see the process, they are learning by osmosis. If you love sewing, share your experiences.

Recently, as part of a fund-raiser, I provided dinner and gave a tour of our historic home. Every room was impeccably tidy, except the third floor (attic), where I have my office and photography and sewing studios. When the guests came downstairs, they asked me if leaving my studio looking "lived in" was intentional...the sewing piles, the book-writing piles and stacks of design ideas. They were fascinated that I didn't mind their seeing work in progress and were sure I had staged it. It made me human and they loved it! AND, most of all, I was NOT embarrassed.

Read this book and be open-minded about where you create your space. Relax your standards if you are fastidiously tidy. Think of your space as the university of sewing. Now, read on for inspiration.

Pati Palmer

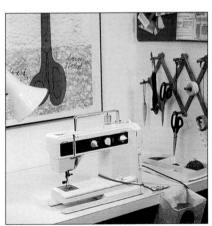

ABOUT THE AUTHOR

A Montana native, Lynette Ranney Black attended Montana State University where she majored in home economics and business. She settled in Portland, Oregon, and in her first job with a sewing machine company.

Black later took her architectural and interior design skills from college and went to work for a kitchen and bath remodeling firm. After seven years she met the requirements to become a Certified Kitchen Designer. During her years in the remodeling/design field, she held many positions in the NW States Chapter of NKBA (National Kitchen and Bath Association), including president.

After the birth of her first child, Black found a need to be home on evenings and weekends, so she returned to the home-sewing industry as promotions manager for Palmer/Pletsch, a publisher specializing in consumer education.

She wrote Palmer/Pletsch's most popular bulletin, *Trends in Sewing Room Design*. Then she co-authored with Linda Wisner a best-selling book, *Creative Serging for the Home and Other Quick Decorating Ideas*. In its first year it sold nearly 100,000 copies and in 1991 won the coveted PCM award for best book of the year in sewing and crafts.

With her background in room design, remodeling and sewing, she now brings us *Dream Sewing Spaces: Design and Organization for Spaces Large and Small*.

ABOUT THIS BOOK

We've all dreamed about it. We've planned it in our mind many times. We've sipped tea, visualized and asked ourselves, "What if?" Then reality steps in and we tell ourselves, "I don't even know where to start." That is where this book comes in. *Dream Sewing Spaces: Design & Organization for Spaces Large & Small* is written to help **you** design **your** space to meet **your** needs.

Unless you live in a grand house with many rooms and open spaces, finding personal space for sewing may seem impossible. But finding the space may simply require a new way of looking at your space and your hobby. We may need to realign our thinking and give our hobby legitimacy. So many times our needs are not recognized, therefore space and money are not dedicated to our sewing. If we have a designated and recognized place in which to sew, we add validity to our hobby and/or livelihood. This doesn't necessarily mean you need a room all to yourself—just a nook may be all you need. Many times, your space may be a section of a room shared with the family...so you can fix a snack, chat with your husband, mend a hurt knee or listen to an upset child.

Wherever it is, you'll want to design it to be as efficient and comfortable as possible. This book starts with analyzing yourself, your needs and the space you have to work with. We'll discuss human energy and how to get the most out of the energy we have. We'll look at possible design layouts and talk about our choices for cabinets, countertops and other surfaces. We'll learn about lighting and electricity so we can finish our sewing-room plan. We'll also look at small sewing spaces and how to use them to the utmost efficiency, and at specialty sewing such as professional dressmakers, quilters, crafters and home decorators and meeting their special needs.

An appendix is included to help you free up storage space by organizing your home's closets and using them to their fullest potential.

Note: For any name-brand product mentioned, the resource section features the manufacturer's or distributor's address and phone number.

FINDING SEWING SPACE

Illustration by Kate Pryka

Spare rooms or no-longer-used rooms. *As children grow up and leave the family home, spare rooms are left! A complete room is generally large enough to handle whatever furniture and equipment you use.*

Attics *An attic can be turned into a wonderful sewing space (see pages 8-9), but be prepared to put a lot of work into creating the space.*

Closets *Oftentimes a closet can be liberated from its current use and creatively reorganized and designed as a fabulous sewing space. (See page 114.)*

Other nooks and crannies. *Don't forget to consider stairway landings, under staircases (see page 103) and basement spaces.*

Most of us are so used to our homes we easily overlook potential sewing space. Examine your home from top to bottom and, while looking at options, consider the following factors.

Is the space adequate in size?

You know you require certain pieces of furniture and equipment. Keep their dimensions in mind as you evaluate possible locations.

Is electrical power adequate?

Your space must have adequate power for your equipment and lighting demands. The most significant consumer of electricity will be the pressing equipment. Be sure the existing wiring is sufficient to handle the extra load, or be prepared to add power.

Is heating, cooling and ventilation adequate?

Obviously this is important for physical comfort and good health. To work at your most efficient level, the room temperature and humidity should be comfortable. An attic space is usually inadequately cooled or ventilated, and basements and garages are often inadequately heated. Plan to upgrade those spaces.

Are there exterior windows?

One or more windows can be a necessity. Nothing beats natural light for sewing...and for mental and physical well-being.

What will the noise level be like?

Quiet is a two-way consideration. Keeping noise confined to the sewing space may be as important as keeping unwanted noise out. Consider the needs of your family, your sewing habits and times, as well as the proximity to bedrooms.

Shared spaces. One of the simplest setups is taking over a portion of an existing room. Perhaps you can appropriate one wall of a bedroom, a section of a family room or laundry room, the dining room's bay window, the end of a hall or the breakfast nook off the kitchen.

Exterior spaces. Perhaps the most promising space is not even in the house! Consider using part or all of the garage or the loft above the garage, wall in a porch or deck, or take over the shed or guest house on the property. However, these spaces usually require a fair amount of remodeling to be usable.

THE INSPIRATION OF DREAMS MADE REAL

The rooms on the next several pages, and on pages 34 to 45 and 88 to 97, started as dreams in the minds of sewers all across the country...and are now a reality. Though your needs, space requirements and availability may be different, look at each space with an open mind and eye. Is there a storage idea or layout style that you particularly like? Would it work in your space?

PATI PALMER'S ATTIC SEWING SPACE

Pati Palmer is founder and CEO of Palmer/Pletsch Publishing. The space shown here is located in the attic of her historic home in Portland, Oregon. Electrical updating was needed, as well as a general brightening with paint. This previously ill-used room now serves as Pati's sewing space and the set of Palmer/Pletsch videos. It's also the research and development area for sewing techniques and the patterns Pati designs for McCall's. For more information about this room see pages 42 and 43.

FAMILY IS IMPORTANT

My office/sewing space is open to the kitchen of my country home. Daughters Kelsey and Jessi can play near, content to have Mom in view. The space was originally designed as a dining room, but a kitchen remodel created plenty of space for the family's dining needs, freeing room for a home office and SEWING! For more on this space see pages 94-97.

...you can have a great sewing space! This compact sewing area has room for both serger and sewing machine, plus plenty of storage for fabric and projects. For how-to details, see pages 100-101. And for suggestions on freeing up a closet for sewing, see Appendix A, page 114.

A DESIGNER'S LOFT

Jo Reimer, fiber artist and designer, planned her new home to include a fabulous loft space above the garage, which overlooks the living room and kitchen. Jo is an amazingly creative woman who enjoys rearranging her space. By designing her space to include a combination of built-in cabinets and movable units, she is not tied to one arrangement. Her studio consists of a series of Techline units used to create an eye-catching storage area, as well as moveable sewing tables, a custom-designed island, and an office area created with cabinets. She completed the space with antiques.

Jo's sewing "L" gives her two views...one of her backyard landscaping and the other of her living room and kitchen.

An office "L" is beyond the sewing space.

As a fiber artist and pattern designer, Jo needed a large planning/ cutting area. A cabinet maker built her generous island to her specifications (see page 26-27 for more information on islands). She also planned two design walls. The one at the far end of the island, next to the closet, is created using Homosote, a building material. The other is a panel of rigid insulation. Because it is covered with a flannel sheet, fabric clings to it beautifully. (See pages 50-51 and 108-109.) The general lighting in her studio is provided with the use of halogen track lights. Jo has rounded out her space with the use of antiques. To see a floor plan of this space, turn to page 27.

Jo's closet is envied by all who see it. The shelves are painted plywood and spaced perfectly for bussing bins (available from restaurant-supply stores). Each bin is labeled with contents.

A SEWING ROOM BETWEEN DINING ROOM AND LAUNDRY

Marta Alto, Palmer/Pletsch corporate educator, may very well be the fastest sewer in the West. Some of her speed is due to her custom-designed sewing space. Marta's home is located in Lake Oswego, Oregon, and is situated to take advantage of a beautiful view of the lake. She claimed her space adjacent to the dining room and kitchen. Located near family activities, she can throw dinner in the oven and keep right on sewing! Marta used some open storage, making it simple and quick to choose thread or interfacing for a project. However, most cabinets are closed, freeing time needed to keep the room tidy. Marta uses many different machines and stores those not in use under the counter in the kneehole spaces. For more information about this room see pages 38-39.

Marta stores her buttons in clear plastic boxes lined up on her windowsill.

At right is a hand-painted clock created by artist Kelley Salber.

SEWING IN THE DINING ROOM

This dining room in a turn-of-the-century home converts easily to very usable sewing space. The 18th century table is just the right height to serve as a rotary cutting surface. (The mat stores behind the piano.) The gate-leg table in the bay window opens to create plenty of sewing surface for the modern machine that is stored behind the sideboard. The sideboard also provides storage for sewing notions, pressing equipment and fabric, as well as the family silver. The old dress form is used to display a rotation of antique dresses when not being put to use for a draping project. The thread cabinet next to it has lots of space for threads, trims, zippers, buttons and other small item storage. (For a close-up of storage details, see pages 4 and 87.)

Gail Brown's collection of antique sewing items becomes accessories in a dining room filled with antiques. Antique pincushions and miniature sewing machines make fascinating conversation pieces. Turn-of-the-century fashion prints hang in the window and on walls. An antique dress form displays the owner's great-grandmother's dress. Fabrics tucked into an oversize basket add rich color as they wait to be turned into sewing projects. All in all, it's a very inviting room to spend time in. Buck the dog thinks so!

## CHAPTER I

ANALYZE YOU, YOUR NEEDS, YOUR SPACE

The "typical" sewer is an illusion. We are all different and the design of our sewing space will be different. Each of the sewing spaces in the photos was created for a unique individual. Each design is determined by that individual's needs and desires.

The first step to creating YOUR custom sewing space is to analyze your needs. Ask yourself questions using the questionnaire beginning on the next page. Think about what kind of sewing you do. Is it a hobby? Do you earn your living sewing? What kind of projects do you work on? What kind of space is required? What tools and equipment do you have? How many people will use the space? Perhaps you and your child sew together!

First, take inventory of all the items that will go into your dream sewing room. Then analyze your body. Learn how you move in and use space. The final step is to analyze the space you have to work with and to begin planning how to use it.

When you are finished with the questionnaire, you might want to look at the photos in the previous section again. Try to figure out what the people are like who work in these rooms. What are their needs?

We remodeled my sewing room this winter... my Christmas present. I went through everything, cleaning and re-organizing. That was almost as fun as sewing! It meant I got to play with everything in my stash and got all inspired again.

Chris

Christine Sloss, Dublin, CA—
a Palmer/Pletsch sewing school workshop graduate
inspired by a sewing room design presentation.

Your Needs

Are you a hobby sewer or a professional?_____
If professional, do clients come to your home?_____
How many people will work in the room?_____

Reason for the question: The more people in the room at a time, the more equipment will be needed and a larger and more spacious space should be allotted.

What type of sewing do you do?
Rate by % of sewing time spent.

Fashion	_____	%
Crafts	_____	%
Home Decorating	_____	%
Quilting	_____	%
Bridal/Formalwear	_____	%
Art to Wear	_____	%
Other	_____	%
	100	%

Reason for the question: Different types of sewing have different needs. For instance, the craft sewer has zillions of little items that need to be stored, so storage and organization are of utmost importance. The actual sewing, cutting, pressing area need not be large or extensive. But the home decorator, quilter and bridal/formalwear sewer need large spaces for dealing with a large amount of fabrics, and storage space must be planned differently. See chapter 9, Specialty Sewing.

Are you a one-at-a-time project person or do you have lots of projects going at one time?

Reason for the question: Multiple projects require organization of the parts and pieces for each project.

Do you sew one-of-a-kind projects, or many of the same items at a time?

Reason for the question: A one-at-a-time, one-of-a-kind project person requires less space dedicated to projects in construction, such as hanging space or project baskets.

Take inventory of your sewing items.
Taking inventory of your possessions will help you visualize your needs and give you concrete measurements to use when designing storage spaces and deciding on organizational tools.

How many machines do you have?
No. of sewing machines _____ No. of sergers _____
Others (e.g. embroidery, commercial, blind hem, etc.) _____

Do you use every machine all the time, or is there a machine you rarely use but must keep?

Reason for the question: The more machines you have, the more space you need. However, if there is a machine you keep just for a particular task, consider storing it under the sewing counter and bring it into commission only when needed.

Do you own a press? How often do you use it? Why do you use it?

Reason for the question: The press, like a microwave in your kitchen, should be placed according to how you use it. If you use it only for interfacing it may be best to store it away and bring it out for use. If you use it all the time, it must be planned into the design. Most use the press in a standing position so it should be placed at a higher height. If you use it while sitting, place it at a lower level.

How much fabric do you have on hand?
Number of bolts _____
Fold and stack the fabric and measure it.
How many inches high? _____ "

How many patterns do you have? _____
Line them up and measure the inches of space needed. _____ "

Are you a "pattern collector"? _____
In your planning, don't forget to allow for growth of your pattern collection.
Do you have the same pattern in many different sizes? _____

How may spools of thread do you have?
Line up and measure the inches of space needed.

# of small spools	_____	inches	_____
# of large spools	_____	inches	_____
# of small tubes	_____	inches	_____
# of large tubes	_____	inches	_____
# of cones	_____	inches	_____
# of king cones	_____	inches	_____

Number of pairs of scissors, shears and rotary cutters_____
List them and their uses_____
_____

Number of sewing and crafts books_____
Line them up and measure the inches of space needed.
_____ " Remember to allow for additional books.

Do you have multiples of the same sewing notion? If so, make a note of them. _____
_____

Are you one to buy every sewing item ever created, or do you make do with what you have?

Reason for the question: The more we know about ourselves the better we can design our space. If we buy every new item on the market, expansion space needs to be planned into our design.

YOUR BODY

Now you need to take some measurements of yourself. You may need a friend's help to ensure accurate measurements.

Reason for the questions: The measurements are necessary for getting the sewing, cutting, and sitting height proper for your body. You need to be familiar with your comfortable reach to aid in determining upper storage placement and countertop depth.

A. What is the measurement from your sitting position to the floor? Sit with feet flat on the floor with no pressure on the back of your legs.

B. How far can you comfortably reach while sitting?

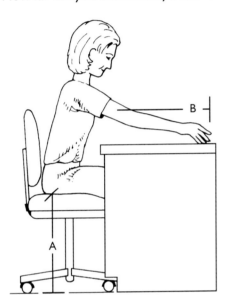

C. What is the measurement from your mid-elbow to the floor?

D. How far can you comfortably reach while standing in front of a 25" deep countertop?

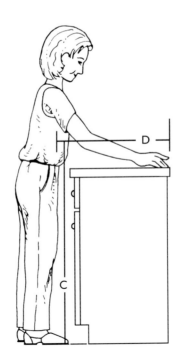

YOUR SPACE

Now that you've taken inventory of your sewing items and taken a look at your own physical measurements, it's time to look at the space you have to work with. It may be a section of the family room or bedroom, or you may be fortunate and have a spare bedroom, converted garage, basement or attic space all to yourself! In any case, measure the space with a metal tape measure. Note where the windows and doors are in the room and any architectural objects, such as plumbing chases, heat ducts, chimneys and posts. The reason for the measuring is to determine the space you have to use, so measure from corner to window or door trim, door trim to trim, window trim to trim and height of window from floor to trim. Also measure the ceiling height and note the location of electrical switches, outlets, and light fixtures.

Using these measurements, draw a **floor plan** of the space and elevations of each wall. Graph paper may help with this task. Use a lightly gridded paper so your lines will show up well. Use a scale of fi inch = 1 foot. (Designers work in this scale; architects work in a 1/4 inch = 1 foot scale.)

A **floor plan** is a bird's-eye view of your room. Pretend you are stuck to the ceiling and looking down at your space. This is a floor plan.

Floor Plan

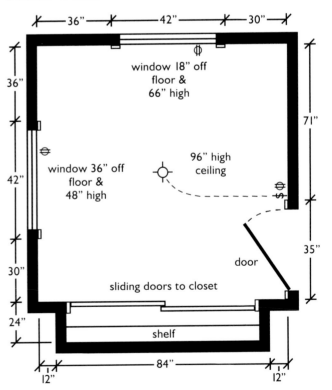

USING TEMPLATES

A head-on view or frontal view is an **elevation**. It shows how a room looks to a person standing in the middle of the floor and looking at one wall. The purpose of an elevation is to allow you to plan room layout in relation to windows, doors, electrical outlets and other architectural objects.

When your sewing space is on paper, it will be easier for you to be objective in planning work and storage stations. If you have existing furniture you plan to use, measure and cut out fi"-scale templates of them to "play" with your layout.

Your layout begins to take shape as you play with the pieces that need to fit into your sewing space. Cut out templates (scale model) of the major elements, then move them around your floor plan to experiment with various layouts.

Architects and designers use standard symbols to indicate certain features on floor plans. They are simple symbols and you will want to use them on your floor plan, especially if you are hiring electrical or construction work, because the symbols add essential information without cluttering the floor plan with written labels. Below are samples of the most common symbols.

Elevations

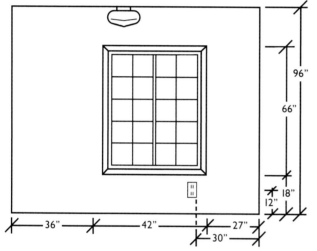

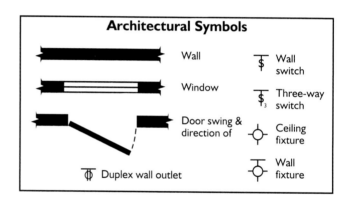

Positioning Elements

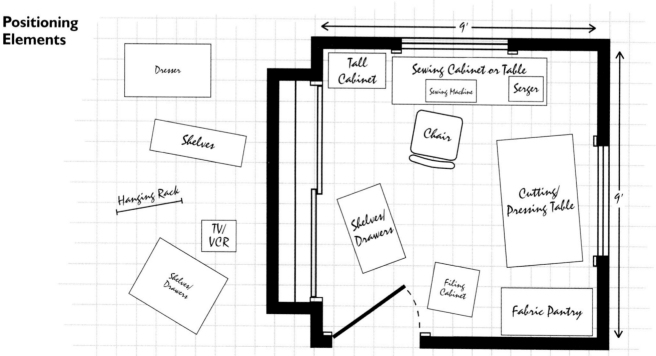

SPACE LAYOUT POSSIBILITIES

ONE-WALL STYLES

The "one-wall" style has the use of only one wall for furniture, cabinets or tall units, but the actual sewing space can be extended farther into the room for temporary use. This is a common style when sharing the space with the family. The sewing machines and all primary storage occur along the wall. Any overflow storage and secondary equipment must find a home elsewhere, such as a bedroom closet, linen closet or under a bed. At right is a compact one-wall sewing area. Below is another idea.

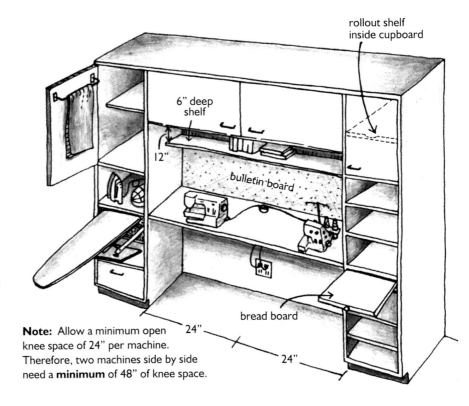

rollout shelf inside cupboard

6" deep shelf

12"

bulletin board

bread board

24"

24"

Note: Allow a minimum open knee space of 24" per machine. Therefore, two machines side by side need a **minimum** of 48" of knee space.

Use a Hallway Linen Closet

Take advantage of an "extra" closet (see Appendix A, page 114, for help in creating an "extra" closet).

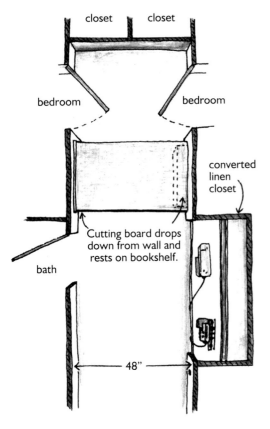

closet   closet

bedroom   bedroom

converted linen closet

Cutting board drops down from wall and rests on bookshelf.

bath

48"

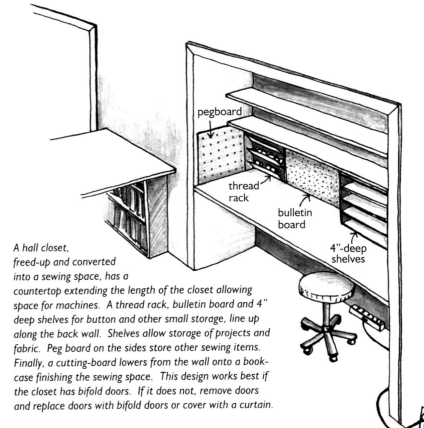

pegboard

thread rack

bulletin board

4"-deep shelves

A hall closet, freed-up and converted into a sewing space, has a countertop extending the length of the closet allowing space for machines. A thread rack, bulletin board and 4" deep shelves for button and other small storage, line up along the back wall. Shelves allow storage of projects and fabric. Peg board on the sides store other sewing items. Finally, a cutting-board lowers from the wall onto a bookcase finishing the sewing space. This design works best if the closet has bifold doors. If it does not, remove doors and replace doors with bifold doors or cover with a curtain.

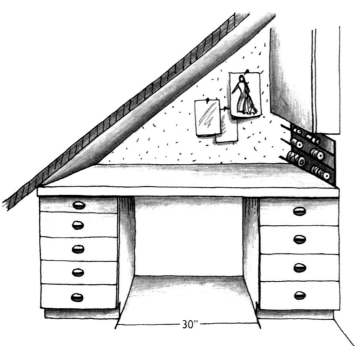

One-Wall Under the Eaves

This drawing shows the use of a small, usually unused area in an attic or corner of a room. A sewing area is created using drawers and a countertop. The cutting surface folds down from the wall and rests on an attached leg.

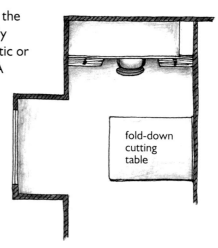

fold-down cutting table

CORRIDOR STYLES

The "corridor" style uses two sections or lines of cabinets with space between. This can be created by using one wall with an island or two parallel walls. The corridor between cabinet sections should be at least 36".

Use a Breakfast Nook

This 6^1/$_2$' square breakfast nook has been recommissioned as a sewing space. Both sides of the nook are lined with cabinets and serve as sewing centers. The press center is simply an ironing board that hangs from a caddy when not in use. Cutting occurs on the dining room table. A simple curtain hung on curtain wire serves as a door.

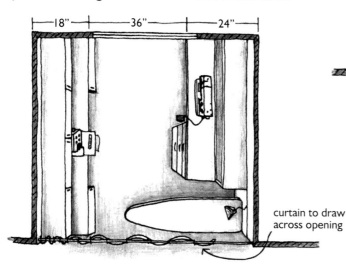

curtain to draw across opening

When There Are No Blank Walls...

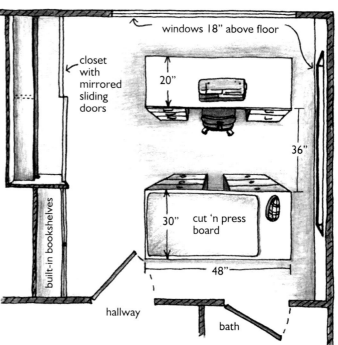

windows 18" above floor

closet with mirrored sliding doors

20"

36"

built-in bookshelves

30" cut 'n press board

48"

hallway

bath

The bedroom above has low windows, two doors, a closet and built-in bookshelves...and so furniture cannot be placed against the walls. Create an island corridor in the middle, leaving at least 18" around the outside edges.

L-Shape

The L-shaped space is a step up in efficiency. It allows you to place a work center on each leg of the "L." A good rolling chair puts a final touch on efficiency.

Note: When creating an L space, you end up with one "dead" corner. There are many ways to use that space. Consider placing a large basket or free-standing shelf or drawer unit in the corner, or use corner cabinetry such as a lazy susan or rotary garbage bins. The bins could be used to store bulky items such as Poly-Fil® or fabric scraps or as a giant button bin! (Just kidding!)

A Corner in a Family Room

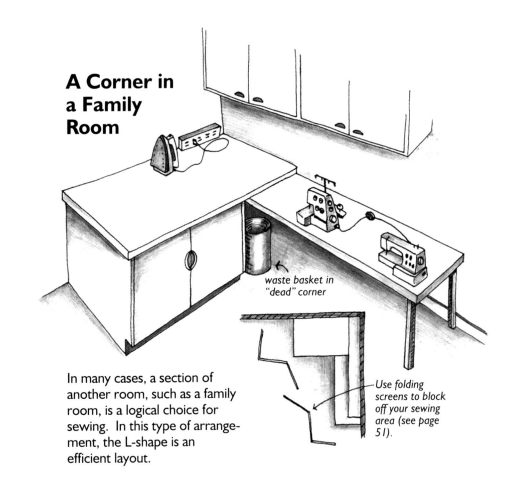

In many cases, a section of another room, such as a family room, is a logical choice for sewing. In this type of arrangement, the L-shape is an efficient layout.

waste basket in "dead" corner

Use folding screens to block off your sewing area (see page 51).

The Corner of a Dining Room

When you use beautifully finished wood cabinets, a sewing space in a dining room can fit right in with your other furniture. To emphasize the furniture look you may want to store the machines inside the cabinets.

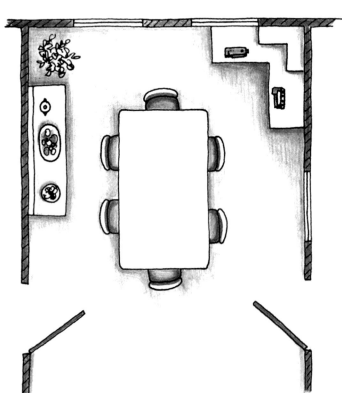

22

The End of a Hallway...

A dead-end hallway provides a cozy and convenient space for a sewing L. This hall is 4' wide. The lower cabinet on the left leg of the L is 18" deep—a great depth for storage. The cabinet above it is 12" deep and has a tambour door behind which the serger is stored. The right leg of the L is a 21" deep sewing center. The "dead" corner houses open storage. Upper cabinets line the wall to add extra storage.

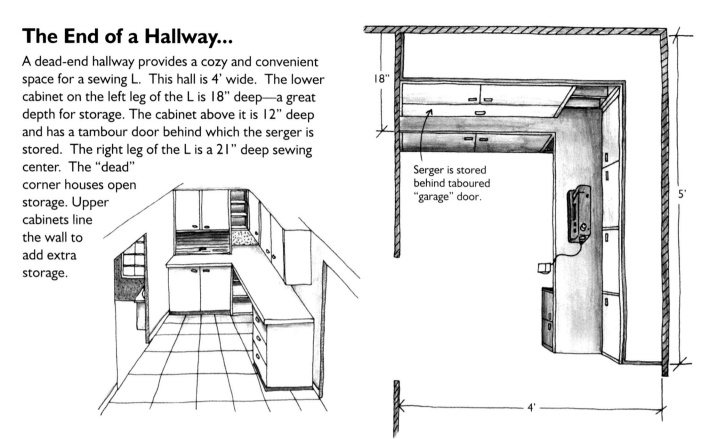

18"

Serger is stored behind taboured "garage" door.

5'

4'

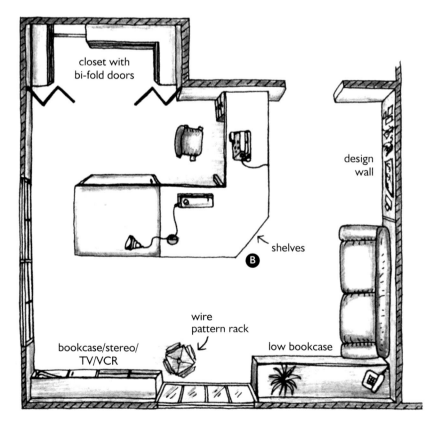

closet with bi-fold doors

design wall

shelves

B

wire pattern rack

bookcase/stereo/ TV/VCR

low bookcase

A Peninsula L

An L doesn't need to follow the walls. This L-shaped peninsula is an ideal work area, with easy access to sewing and storage areas. Efficient space was created by incorporating the closet storage area into the primary work space.

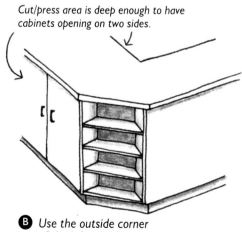

Cut/press area is deep enough to have cabinets opening on two sides.

B *Use the outside corner of the L for shelf storage.*

23

U-Shape

As in a kitchen, a U shape may be the most efficient layout. The U allows you to have all work centers within easy reach of the rolling chair.

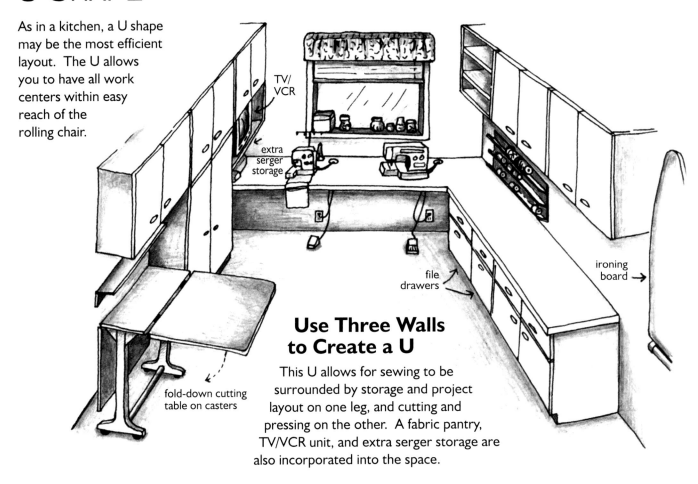

TV/VCR

extra serger storage

file drawers

ironing board

fold-down cutting table on casters

Use Three Walls to Create a U

This U allows for sewing to be surrounded by storage and project layout on one leg, and cutting and pressing on the other. A fabric pantry, TV/VCR unit, and extra serger storage are also incorporated into the space.

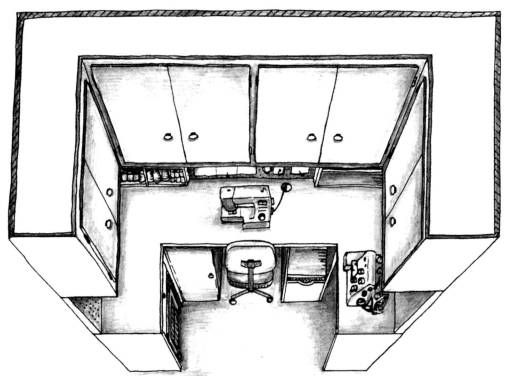

A Sewing Cubby in a 4' x 8' Butler's Pantry

This tiny space's previous life was as a butler's pantry. Now it is a small but efficient sewing space. Lining the walls with wall cabinets greatly expands storage (and the cabinets may already be there). The space between wall cabinets and the counter top is efficiently used by adding narrow shelves for thread and small storage, pegboard for notion storage, and a bulletin board.

Combine an L with Additional Work Space to Create a U

Meridith Piatt of Ft. Myers, Florida, created an efficient, yet comfortable, sewing space. The L sewing center shares the end of one leg with a pressing center. The cutting center is a special folding table (see page 63). An appealing tall unit was added to the room, with open shelves to house the TV/VCR unit and decorative items, and closed doors for fabric and 'messy' storage. The window seats serve as pattern storage and also as a "landing" spot for her husband. (His books and magazines are stored in a 12" deep cabinet facing the left window seat—this cabinet also serves as support for the countertop.) The "extra" cabinet and counter surface between the windows were planned for growth—perhaps an embroidery machine will sit there, or a press, or . . .

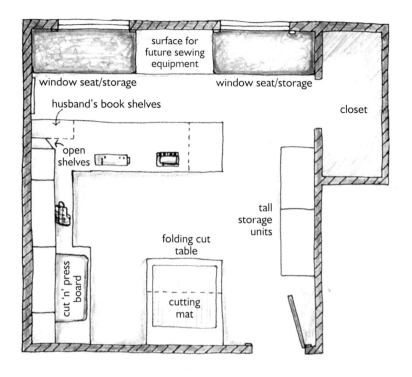

surface for future sewing equipment

window seat/storage

window seat/storage

closet

husband's book shelves

open shelves

tall storage units

folding cut table

cut 'n' press board

cutting mat

ISLAND VARIATION

You may have been dreaming of an island kitchen; now dream of an island sewing space. The island variation can be used with any of the before-mentioned shapes and is guaranteed to increase efficiency. Often the island is used as a cut and/or press center due to its accessibility to all sides, but it can also be used for sewing machines.

This is especially suitable for the home decorator, quilter and other sewers who deal with stitching large pieces. The island can also double as a storage unit. **When planning, be sure to allow a minimum of 36" for an aisle between the island and any other object.**

The island may be nothing more than a table. Or it could be created out of cabinets. If the island will be used for cutting and pressing, the minimum size should be 30" x 48". This size allows for laying out a 1fi yard length of 60"-wide fabric folded in half.

Graphic designer Linda Wisner chose to use an extendable oak table as a multi-use island in her compact studio. The table serves as a planning area and cut/press center, as well as conference table and layout area for her design work. See page 93 for more information on Linda's studio.

Professional dressmaker and international speaker Kathleen Spike created a large cutting island by using a 4' x 8' sheet of top-quality plywood. She padded the plywood with army blankets then covered the entire surface with cotton duck cloth. The covered plywood was placed on top of an unused table. She added storage below the surface through the use of rolling wire-basket systems. See page 105 for more information on this space.

↖ *open space to store the cutting mats*

Palmer/Pletsch corporate educator Marta Alto created a cut/press island using standard kitchen cabinets. Her island consists of a three-drawer unit, which houses patterns in the two deep drawers and a pull-out ironing board in one small drawer, and two open wall cabinets, which she raised with toe kicks. These three cabinets are joined with a painted wood countertop on which she places her cut 'n' press board. She added a 6" high and deep cubby to hold her pressing equipment and to raise the iron off the countertop. See pages 38-39 for more about Marta's space.

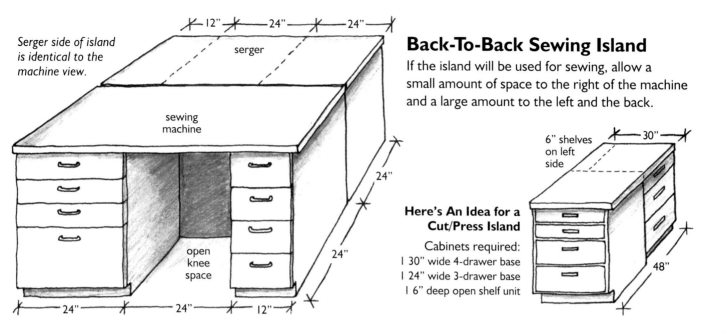

Serger side of island is identical to the machine view.

12" — 24" — 24"

serger

sewing machine

open knee space

24"

24"

24"

24" — 24" — 12"

Back-To-Back Sewing Island

If the island will be used for sewing, allow a small amount of space to the right of the machine and a large amount to the left and the back.

6" shelves on left side

30"

48"

Here's An Idea for a Cut/Press Island

Cabinets required:
1 30" wide 4-drawer base
1 24" wide 3-drawer base
1 6" deep open shelf unit

THE ULTIMATE...

Jo Reimer has the true dream sewing space...a generous loft with a combination of U, L, island and one-wall sewing, storage and office areas. Even her closet is an efficiently designed U. For more photos of Jo's space, see pages 12 and 13.

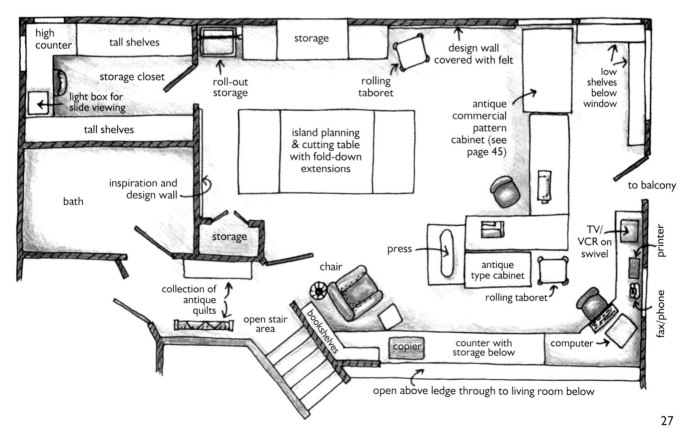

high counter

tall shelves

storage closet

light box for slide viewing

tall shelves

bath

inspiration and design wall

storage

collection of antique quilts

open stair area

bookshelves

chair

copier

roll-out storage

island planning & cutting table with fold-down extensions

rolling taboret

press

antique type cabinet

rolling taboret

storage

design wall covered with felt

antique commercial pattern cabinet (see page 45)

low shelves below window

to balcony

TV/ VCR on swivel

printer

fax/phone

computer

counter with storage below

open above ledge through to living room below

CHAPTER 2

HUMAN ENERGY

Before we go further into the layout of the sewing space, let's consider the human body, its spendable energy, and how to design to make the best use of both.

We all have many demands on our precious 24 hours in a day. To fulfill necessary demands and still have energy left for sewing, we need to learn to manage our energy. Unfortunately energy management is more difficult to get a handle on than time management, because we vary in the amount of spendable energy we each have, depending on our genetics, mental health and physical health.

Sewing requires several types and combinations of efforts. **Mental effort** is needed to organize and complete even the simplest of projects. **Visual effort** is constantly required—the eye directs the movements of the body. **Manual effort** is any reaching, pulling or pushing action performed while sewing, including bending, leaning, rising, turning, stooping, sitting, and kneeling. Also, **pedal effort** (walking, moving, and standing) is an essential part of most activities.

Energy is expended during all aspects of sewing. To make the most of your energy, it is important to not stay frozen in one position or posture for extended periods. Plan to alternate between the sitting and standing work stations for sewing (and computing) every 15 minutes. Changing your stance can effectively renew your energy, plus relax your muscles and temperament. Don't forget to blink (to help prevent eye fatigue), stretch, shake your hands and rotate your shoulders about every 30 minutes.

Today's manufacturers are incorporating a concept called ergonomics into designing sewing equipment and tools. **Ergonomics** is defined as "the science of coordinating the design of tools, equipment and furniture with the capabilities and requirements of the user's comfort and convenience, health and safety, as well as pleasure and satisfaction." Ergonomics deals with proper work heights for sitting and standing; the design of furniture and equipment such as scissors, cutters, chairs, sewing machines and sergers; and lighting and color. What it comes down to is, every

thing you touch, hold and operate when sewing should have some ergonomic features.

Work and Storage Centers

There are three primary "centers" to be included in every sewing space. They are the sewing center, the cut/press center and the storage center. As space allows, and depending on the type of sewing you do, additional secondary centers are needed: a fitting area, hanging area and planning. For ideas on creating these centers, see Chapter 6, Primary and Secondary Work Centers.

SEWING CENTER

This center revolves around sewing machines and sergers and is where all machine sewing occurs.

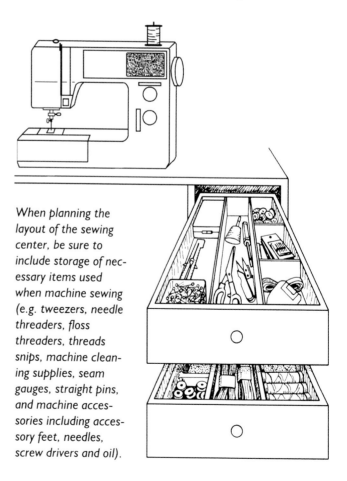

When planning the layout of the sewing center, be sure to include storage of necessary items used when machine sewing (e.g. tweezers, needle threaders, floss threaders, threads snips, machine cleaning supplies, seam gauges, straight pins, and machine accessories including accessory feet, needles, screw drivers and oil).

The Chair

The sewing station also includes the all-important chair. This is an item you do not want to scrimp on. Buy the best ergonomically designed chair you can afford. After all, you will be developing a very close relationship with it. (Your body will thank you.)

It would be easier to sit in a conventional chair if our bodies were square, but alas, they are not. We are designed with curves and bends of different sizes and shapes. Ideally, a chair should fit and support your unique body. Buy one that lets you adjust and modify it to fit **you**.

The seat of a well-designed chair will have a seat pan of about 16" in depth, and the front edge will gently curve down to eliminate the possibility of a decrease in circulation to the lower legs and feet. (Shallower than 16" in depth may not give the needed support to the thighs.) For sewing, the seat pan should be tilted forward up to 15 degrees so the thighs can angle downward, keeping the natural curves of your spine and reducing pressure on your thighs. The seat height should be **adjustable while seated** and range from 14" to 21" from the floor.

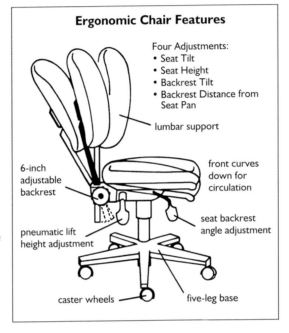

Ergonomic Chair Features

Four Adjustments:
• Seat Tilt
• Seat Height
• Backrest Tilt
• Backrest Distance from Seat Pan

lumbar support

6-inch adjustable backrest

front curves down for circulation

pneumatic lift height adjustment

seat backrest angle adjustment

caster wheels

five-leg base

The back of the chair should be 6" to 9" tall, adjustable both up and down, backward and forward and should be contoured for lumbar support. Lumbar (lower back) support helps you maintain good posture and equalizes the amount of pressure on the spine. Also, the chair should have a five-leg base for the best stability and be on the best-quality casters possible. Try the chair in the store to test the casters, adjustability, and how well the seat swivels from one task to another.

Note: Try to keep your shoulders and hips evenly aligned with each other when twisting or swiveling from one task to another. Never pick up a heavy book or object while the body is twisted. Your back will thank you with years of service if you just treat it right!

Work Height

The industry standard for the height from the floor to the bed of the sewing machine (actual level of sewing) is 29" to 30" off the floor. To check this height on your body, sit in your chair with your feet flat on the floor and knees at a 90-degree angle, bend your elbows at a 90-degree angle and have a friend measure from the floor to the middle of your elbow. The **bed** of your machine should be at this height. (If you completed the **Your Body** section of the questionnaire in chapter one, you already have this measurement.) Fine-tune the fit by using the chair's height adjustability to create the **ideal** angles for your arms, elbows, wrists and hands. You'll know it's right when your body parts do not ache after sewing for long periods.

If you are planning simply to set your machine on a counter, the finished height of the countertop should be 26" to 28" depending on your sewing machine. Take your ideal height measurement and subtract the height of the machine base from the finished height of countertop.

Work Depth

Try to plan a counter depth of 25". This depth is much more comfortable and convenient than the 18" to 21" used by most sewing cabinet companies.

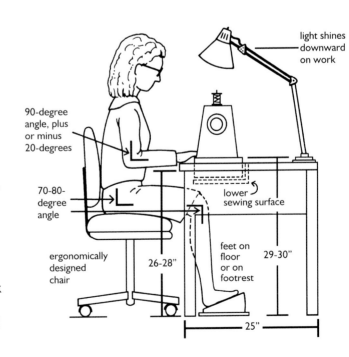

light shines downward on work

90-degree angle, plus or minus 20-degrees

70-80-degree angle

lower sewing surface

ergonomically designed chair

26-28"

feet on floor or on footrest

29-30"

25"

CUT/PRESS CENTER

A multitude of activities takes place at the cut/press center including steam shrinking of fabric, pattern layout, cutting, fusing interfacing, and pressing while sewing.

This center needs to include storage of all pressing supplies such as the June Tailor board, ham, sleeve roll, sleeve boards, point presser, clapper, press cloths and iron, as well as fabric shears, paper scissors, rotary cutters, rotary cutting mats, fabric weights, chalk markers, fabric markers, tracing paper and wheels, rulers, tape measures, straight pins, notepad and pencil.

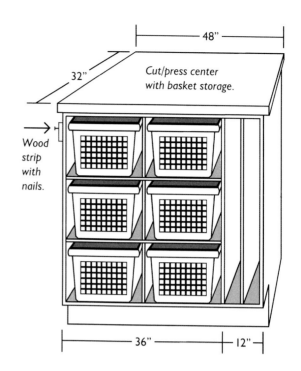

Cut/press center with basket storage.

Wood strip with nails.

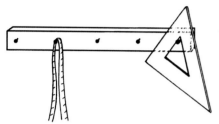

A wood strip with nails or cup hooks or a stemware holder works well for rulers, tape measures, etc.

Work Height at the Cut/Press Center

Work at the cut/press center is usually done in the standing position. Good posture is of vital importance in avoiding strain, limiting fatigue and minimizing energy expenditure. A good standing posture will have the head, neck, chest and abdomen balanced vertically, which enables the spine and bony framework to carry the weight. This posture minimizes the effort and strain placed on the muscles and ligaments. Be conscious of your body. Don't stand for long periods—change

positions. If you must stand for extended periods, look into the various mats and options developed for cushioning the feet.

To determine the proper surface height for you, stand erect with elbows at 90° and lower arms parallel to floor or a bit lower. The correct height for the press center and cutting center (if shears are used for cutting) will be minus 3-4" from the floor-to-mid-elbow dimension. The correct height for rotary cutting will be 6-8" less than this measurement.

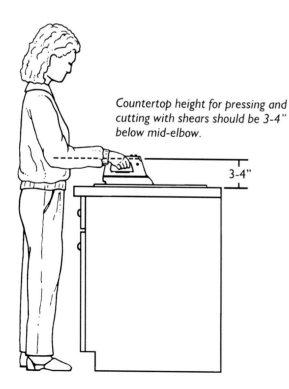

Countertop height for pressing and cutting with shears should be 3-4" below mid-elbow.

3-4"

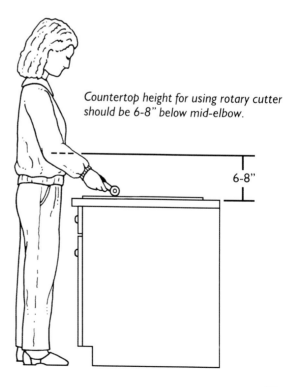

Countertop height for using rotary cutter should be 6-8" below mid-elbow.

6-8"

STORAGE STATIONS

Many studies have been done about human energy and how it relates to storage. From these studies basic storage principles have been developed. Keep them in mind while planning your storage areas.

Basic Storage Principles

1. **Store items at the point of first use.** Each center should include storage of every item used in that location (e.g. the **cut/press center** stores the shears, pressing equipment, pins, markers, etc.).

2. **Store items in multiple locations if used for different tasks.** Some notions are needed at more than one center, including pins, seam gauges and scissors. Therefore, invest in extras and place at all necessary centers.

3. **Items used together should be stored together.** For example, store the glue gun, glue sticks, staple gun and staples together.

4. **Stored items should be easy to locate at a glance.** See Chapter 7, Storage and Organization.

5. **Like articles should be stored or grouped together.** For example, all interfacings should be stored in the same area, all same type of thread together, all fabric paints and markers together, etc.

6. **Frequently used items should be stored within easy reach.** Easy reach is defined as between eye-level and hip-level depending on whether you are standing or sitting.

7. **Items should be easy to grasp at point of storage.** Try to avoid "nesting" or stacking items.

8. **Items should be easily removed without removing other items first.** Give shelf depth careful thought when planning storage space.

9. **Heavy equipment should be stored near the floor.** This is mainly a safety concern. Heavy or bulky items stored on a high shelf could accidentally fall while you are removing them or in an earthquake!

10. **All space should be utilized for utmost efficiency.** Consider cabinet accessories to help with space utilization—especially the deeper base cabinets. Roll-out bottom shelves will help with the efficiency of storage areas below 24" from the floor.

drawer slide

Note: The "two-year test" is a good rule of thumb even for sewing items. If an item hasn't been used in two years, perhaps it should be discarded or given away, rather than stored in valuable space. This is especially true if you are limited to a small space. If you are a teacher, consider whether the item would be of interest in later years. Pati Palmer uses her "notion gimmicks", such as her "Rube Goldberg"-style crotch depth measuring tool, as a part of sewing history to amuse her students.

Prime Storage Levels

Cornell University studied 200 women to determine functional limits for storage areas.

For the medium group of 5'3" to 5'7" (5' 4¾" is the average height of American women) the highest unobstructed average reach is 79". Therefore, the last shelf should be no higher than 72" off the floor. When the reach is over a countertop of 25" in depth, it is reduced to 69", with the last shelf being placed at 66".

While standing, the average woman can easily reach 48" from side to side and 24" off the floor.

While sitting the normal reach curve or elbow circle has a maximum depth of 16". If countertop depth is 25", the extra 9" can be used for storage as well as fabric support while sewing.

When planning the storage center, this study can be used as a guideline for efficient energy use.

Prime storage when we are standing is from knee level to reach level (72") with the least amount of energy used at 48" off the floor. Frequently used items should be stored within this area.

Prime storage while sitting is from knee level to 48".

For dozens of storage ideas see Chapter 7, Storage and Organization.

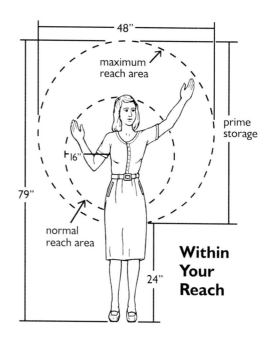

maximum reach area

prime storage

16"

79"

normal reach area

24"

Within Your Reach

Sitting Reach

Frequent Use Area — Place items most often used within the 16" curve.

Occasional Use Area

Storage Only Area

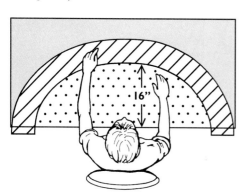

16"

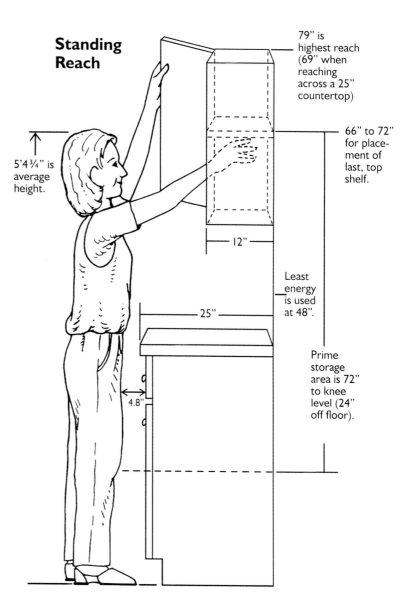

Standing Reach

79" is highest reach (69" when reaching across a 25" countertop)

66" to 72" for placement of last, top shelf.

5'4¾" is average height.

12"

Least energy is used at 48".

25"

4.8"

Prime storage area is 72" to knee level (24" off floor).

33

*Roberts
sewing cabinet*

## CHAPTER 3

CABINETRY AND OTHER FURNITURE

Cabinetry is one of the most important elements in your sewing space. The placement of the cabinets and other furniture creates the layout of the sewing space.

Many feasible options are available. Choose from free-standing furniture, kitchen and bath cabinetry, or office and computer furniture.

FREE-STANDING SEWING FURNITURE

Special cabinetry designed for sewing has come a long way in recent years. Ergonomics (the study of the relationship between you and your work space) has been applied to many of the sewing cabinets. Sewing cabinets are available from local sewing machine dealers or in some cases, directly from the manufacturer (see Resource Section), and come in a variety of sizes, styles, and designs. You can choose contemporary or traditional door styles and traditional or European construction.

Traditional construction means the case of the cabinet is made with a visible frame around the door (face frame), while European construction is face frameless.

Sewing cabinets are manufactured to certain industry standards and are created with the sewing machine and its operator in mind. These cabinets are free-standing, not permanently attached to the wall, and

are treated like a piece of furniture. Most cabinets housing the sewing machine come with lifts to raise and lower the machine. They easily convert from free arm to flatbed.

Depending on your needs, you can purchase just one unit (perhaps a cabinet to house your sewing machine) or a series of units. These cabinets sport many extra goodies such as built-in storage trays, drop-leaf shelves for extra counter space when sewing, flip-up ironing boards or ironing boards in drawers, built-in thread racks, serger shelves, magazines racks, bulletin boards and pegboards.

A few companies (see next page) offer quite a selection of cabinet sizes, shapes and styles, allowing you to arrange them into an efficient layout for your space, and at least one company offers a design service that helps you design your sewing space.

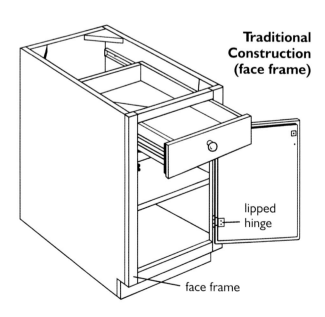

Traditional Construction (face frame)

lipped hinge

face frame

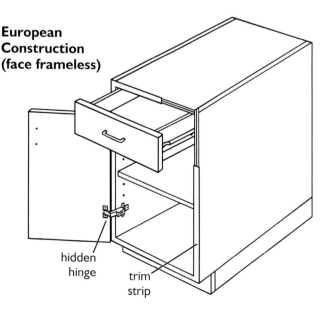

European Construction (face frameless)

hidden hinge

trim strip

Free-Standing Sewing Furniture

J.T. Parsons Cabinet Company built this 34"x 20"x 31" unit at right (model #8002). It features four storage drawers, thread rack, a beautiful oak finish and an electric sewing machine lift.

Ritter Manufacturing builds a complete line of modular units for the sewing space. The photo above shows some of these units in action. Ritter also offers a design service to help you plan your space. All units are European construction.

Horn of America builds the creative unit shown at right. It is of European construction and features spool trays, pocket tray, two drawers, a lift for the sewing machine, and an open-out serger table. The unit folds down to a compact size, and when open creates a large sewing surface.

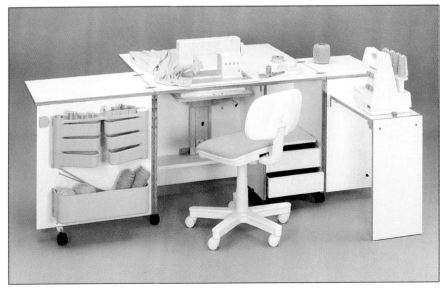

KITCHEN AND BATH CABINETRY

Your dream sewing space may be available through your local kitchen and bath company. Cabinets from the kitchen and bath dealer offer an extensive variety in sizes and styles, allow for a deeper work surface as needed, and offer endless arrangement and storage possibilities. Like your kitchen and bathroom cabinets, these cabinets are installed—meaning they are attached to the walls. This built-in feature offers the most stability for vibration-free sewing and serging. Three basic types of cabinets are available—modular, custom and mod-custom.

The best way to find a reliable dealer is by asking friends and relatives who have recently remodeled a kitchen or bath. Or look in the yellow pages of your telephone directory under kitchen remodel or cabinets. While talking with the salesperson/designer, ask yourself if you feel comfortable with them and are communicating well with them. Ask to see work in progress and completed work the company has done.

Modular Cabinets

Modular Cabinets are usually less expensive than custom cabinets. They are manufactured in specific widths (every 3" increments), depths and heights, and are designed for use in the kitchen, bathroom and desk/office area.

Kitchen Cabinets come in three basic types:

Base cabinets are the bottom cabinets on which the countertop rests. The standard base cabinet is 24" deep, 36" finished height with the countertop and 9" to 48" wide.

Wall cabinets are the upper cabinets, which are hung on the wall. They are 9" to 48" wide, 12" to 42" tall and 12" deep.

Tall cabinets are floor-to-ceiling or almost-ceiling units. They are commonly available in widths of 12" to 42", heights of 84" to 96", and depths of 12" to 24".

Bathroom Cabinets are commonly available in base units only. They are 12" to 48" wide, 18" to 21" deep and 32" to 33" finished height with the countertop.

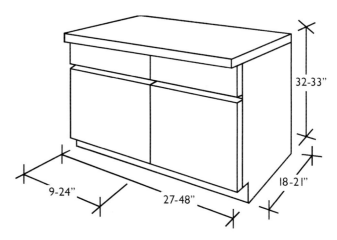

Desk or **Office Cabinets** are not as widely available, but are offered by some modular cabinet companies. They are usually 24" deep, 28" to 30" high with the countertop, and 12" to 30" wide.

Note: These measurements may vary from one cabinet company to another.

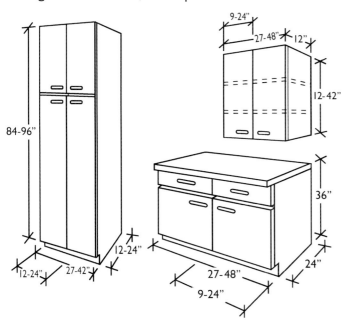

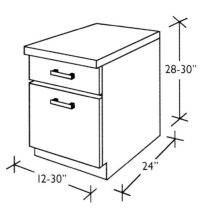

Marta Alto designed her space six years ago and used modular cabinets purchased from a local kitchen and bath showroom. Marta chose the sleek clean lines of laminate cabinets of European construction. She left some cubbyholes without doors in order to store extra-deep interfacing and awkward rotary cutting mats.

Marta is an internationally known corporate educator for Palmer/Pletsch Publishing and a contributing author of many Palmer/Pletsch books. She is an excellent teacher and the star of several Palmer/Pletsch videos including the four serger videos that were shot in her studio.

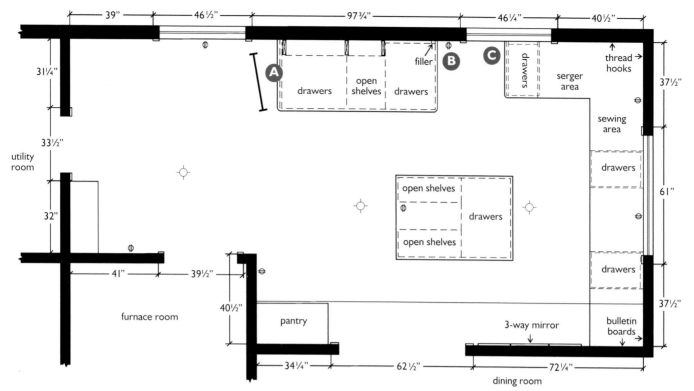

Marta's Sewing Room Floorplan

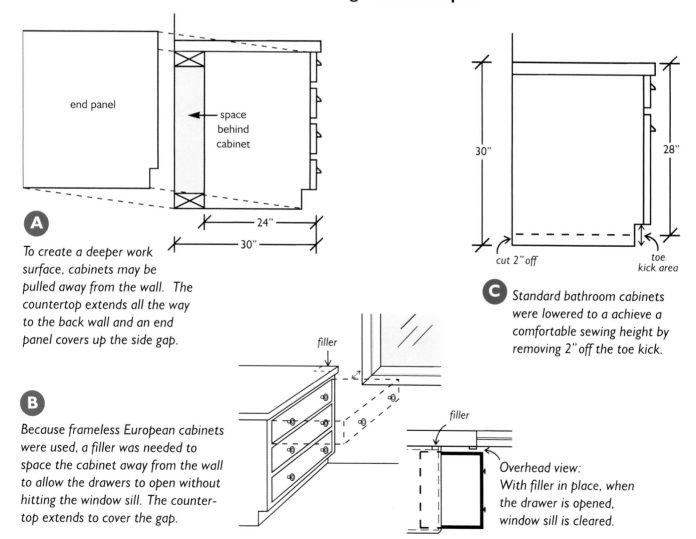

A

To create a deeper work surface, cabinets may be pulled away from the wall. The countertop extends all the way to the back wall and an end panel covers up the side gap.

B

Because frameless European cabinets were used, a filler was needed to space the cabinet away from the wall to allow the drawers to open without hitting the window sill. The countertop extends to cover the gap.

C

Standard bathroom cabinets were lowered to a achieve a comfortable sewing height by removing 2" off the toe kick.

Overhead view: With filler in place, when the drawer is opened, window sill is cleared.

Custom Kitchen and Bath Cabinetry

Custom cabinets can be made to any specifications you wish. These cabinets are available through the kitchen/bath showroom or directly through a cabinet maker. Custom units allow you to have special heights, depths or widths. You can also have special door styles made. Custom cabinets offer you the most variety, but are generally more expensive than modular units.

Mary Mulari is owner of Mary's Productions in Aurora, Minnesota. She is best known for her creative sewing books on appliqué, embellishing sweatshirts, and creating travel gear. Mary is a popular speaker who travels nationwide, giving informative and motivational seminars.

Mary kept resale of the house in mind when she designed her studio and chose a custom cabinet builder to create just the right room for her. A local carpenter used oak to build the cabinets and installed them so they are removable, making it easy to turn the room back into a bedroom.

The SEWING PARLOUR sign hangs above the closet, which has sliding wood doors. In half the closet Mary installed shelving, leaving the hanging rod in place (making it easier to convert back into a standard closet). Mary uses Rubbermaid boxes with labels to organize her storage. On the front sliding door she has mounted a fabric-covered section of Styrofoam insulation to serve as a bulletin board (see page 50).

As a leader in the sewing industry, Mary needs to keep updated on new machines so she designed her space to incorporate two moveable sewing surfaces. These two units are on casters allowing her to pull the units away from the wall, unplug machines and plug in new ones. Mary's cutting table is a Create-a-Space (see page 63) and stores in the corner of the room next to the closet. Mary added warmth and comfort to her room by using wood cabinets, stenciling a border on the wall and hanging a window valance to soften the windows. Honeycombed Duette blinds provide privacy and light reflectance. Open shelves display her button collection in a variety of old canning jars and button boxes. Baskets hold miscellaneous stuff while adding ambiance to the room. Mary's collection of toy sewing machines decorate the top of the tall cabinets. Mary and her husband, Barry, own a sporting goods store with a variety of fishing tackle boxes which, she finds great for storing sewing supplies. (See page 82 in the chapter on storage.)

69"   45"   41½"

open shelves on cupboard base

sewing area   20"

bookshelves set on counters

62"   57"

45½"

These two units are on casters.

24"

60"

closet

20"

49"

serger area

37"

47"

drawers with bookshelves set on top

53"

office

Mod-Custom Cabinetry

Modular-custom (mod-custom) cabinets are cabinets based on modular sizing, but the manufacturer can accommodate some changes (for an upcharge or, in layman's terms, additional cost). These cabinets are not mass-produced like modular units, but are built when the order is received. The machinery is programmed to produce cabinets to the modular specifications for width, height and depth.

Depth modifications in cabinets without drawers are the easiest to do and therefore, the least costly. Depth changes in cabinets with drawers are possible. Extreme height changes can be made by removing the top drawer of a cabinet. This affects only the top bracing. Removing the bottom drawer affects toe-kick configuration which in turn affects end panels and leveling legs.

Pati Palmer's sewing studio was designed for multiple uses: her personal sewing space, sample making and product testing as well as for filming videos. Pati is president of the 20-year-old company, Palmer/Pletsch Publishing. She is an avid fashion sewer; designs patterns for McCall Pattern Co.; is the author of many down-to-earth, easy-to-understand books on fashion sewing; and is an internationally renowned sewing educator.

She chose mod-custom cabinets to create her studio and purchased them through a kitchen and bath dealer. The cabinet manufacturer built the cabinets using vanity-cabinet heights and kitchen-cabinet depths.

The installer dropped the height another two inches by cutting down the toe kicks. The window seats were created by using the drawer cabinet intended to go below a drop-in range. These drawers store Pati's pattern collection.

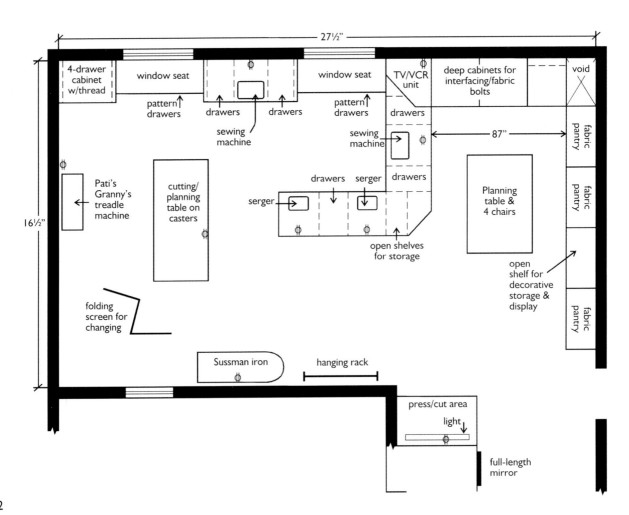

Extra deep (30") cabinets were built to hold bolts of interfacing and fabric. The cabinet company cut the height of the tall cabinets to fit under the sloping ceiling of Pati's attic.

Pati planned for just enough open storage to add ambiance to her space, but not too much to require constant attention to its neatness. Good general lighting was achieved with full-spectrum fluorescent lights.

Pati chose white as her major surface color and loves its light reflectance. She added warmth with wall decorations and storage, pillows, cushions and window valances.

Other Furniture Options

Keep an open mind when looking to furnish your sewing space. Consider looking at furniture designed for other uses—office/computer set-ups, bedrooms, family rooms, garages or workrooms.

Visit your local office supply stores for desk and computer set-ups. Furniture that has a dropped area for the computer keyboard will be the correct height for sewing. Typewriter or printer carts or tables may also work in the sewing center.

Your local building supply store carries a variety of easy-to-assemble units, enabling you to mix and match as needed. Debra Justice purchased units and pre-made countertops to create the sewing and planning areas from a local building supply store. Linda Wisner got her knock-down storage units at a home & garden center.

Techline is a brand of cabinets/furniture available in a good selection of sizes and styles. They are excellent quality and well-designed. Because Techline cabinets are not built-in (they are screwed to each other for stability), they offer flexibility as your space needs change. Jo Reimer used Techline cabinets to create a fabulous storage wall. She also purchased Techline office tables to use as her sewing center.

Techline units form a storage wall for Jo Reimer (above). Taborets from an art supply store serve her design wall.

Units purchased from a building supply store create Debra Justice's space (right and page 91) and the storage wall in Linda Wisner's studio (below).

Antiques

For the antique lover, the proper antiques can create a unique, yet efficient, sewing space. For the sewing space that must be part of other living areas in the home, the use of antiques helps to make the space interesting and livable.

Barbara Weiland, former editor of Sew News and former instructor for Palmer/Pletsch, currently writes for Sew News and writes and edits quilting books. She has sewn on this antique "Hoosier"-type cabinet for years. She augments it with other usable antiques such as a large trunk for fabric storage and printers' drawers for thread.

Jo Reimer, fiber artist and designer, found two fabulous antiques at a yard sale...this old Butterick pattern cabinet (below) and the complete printer's cabinet (bottom left). See pages 12-13 for more on Jo's loft space.

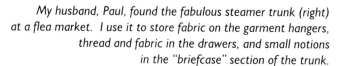

My husband, Paul, found the fabulous steamer trunk (right) at a flea market. I use it to store fabric on the garment hangers, thread and fabric in the drawers, and small notions in the "briefcase" section of the trunk.

Additional antiques can be seen in the dining room on page 15 and in the photos on page 87.

46

## CHAPTER 4

ALL THOSE SURFACES

In addition to the cabinets, there are many surfaces to consider in the sewing space: countertops, floors, walls and ceilings. Each must be scrutinized for durability, practicality, and light reflectance.

FLOORING

As with countertops, your choice of flooring must be practical and easy to keep clean. The floor provides little light reflectance, so a darker color is OK. Medium colors hide the most sins (dust, scratches, thread snips).

Vinyl Flooring

Vinyl can be one of the best flooring choices. It is available in a variety of styles, colors and patterns. Buy the best quality you can afford. Some brands of sheet vinyl come 12' wide so you may not need a seam. If your floor plan does require a seam, however, do not place it in high traffic areas or where your chair will roll over it constantly. Vinyl flooring also comes in 12" squares for easy installation by the do-it-yourselfer— but often every joint becomes a dirt collector. Still, vinyl tile offers the advantage of easy repair if the floor is damaged—simply replace a square or two. Inlaid vinyl flooring (the color goes all the way through the flooring rather than being only on the surface) is more expensive, but may be easily repaired by sanding.

Two additional flooring materials are worth considering—linoleum and rubber. Sheet linoleum, making a strong comeback, is durable and available in several colors and patterns. Rubber is available in tiles and makes for an interesting floor!

Due to continuing advances in technology, there may be something new and exciting you'll want to use in your dream sewing space! Ask your flooring sales associate to tell you what is new.

Hardwood Floors

Hardwood flooring is a popular choice, especially when the sewing space is shared with other activities in the home. It is easy to maintain—just vacuum or dust mop. But it can be damaged by runaway pins stuck under the chair casters. Invest in a few magnetic pin-cushions for rounding up pins and holding them secure. To avoid risk of damage, lay a large section of sheet vinyl or commercial-grade carpet to cover the main work area. This protects, yet is easy to remove as desired. Hardwood flooring can be expensive to install, or you can choose prefinished parquet-style tiles to install yourself—but they tend to collect dirt in the joints just like vinyl tiles. Also available now are tongue-and-groove tiles. A true tongue-and-groove floor is sanded and finished after installation, thus sealing the gaps. If you have a wood floor that is old and splintering, sand and finish with a polyurethane finish rather than wax. Polyurethane keeps moisture from permeating the wood.

Carpet

Carpeting is warm, comfortable to stand on and sound deadening. The best kind for the sewing space is commercial-grade low, dense cut-pile carpet with little or no pad. Such a low-profile carpet will allow easy retrieval of lost pins while plush fibers grab them and refuse to let go! Before deciding on a carpet, drop pins on the samples and see how easily they pick up with the vacuum. (However, pins are hard on a vacuum cleaner. Pick up as many as possible before vacuuming.) Also check how your chair rolls on the carpet. Try, try, try, not to use a plastic chair mat. The edge is always in an inconvenient location. It is a Murphy's Law of sewing! For the do-it-yourselfer, carpet squares work well and have the added benefit of providing a 12" rule on the floor for quick yardage estimating.

Ceramic Tile

Ceramic tile is pretty and has great character, but it doesn't lend itself to a sewing space. It is a hard surface and makes for sore legs and feet if you stand on it very long, and it has no sound absorption whatsoever. If you must have tile, look for flat, larger-size tiles where grout lines are minimal. "Puffy", rounded tiles with large grout lines are hard to clean (grout loves thread snips) and hamper your chair's movement.

COUNTERTOPS

Countertop surface material should be smooth and durable with a matte (not glossy) finish. When choosing the color, consider those in the light to medium range for light reflectance. Check the chart on page 53 for color ideas.

The most practical material and the best choice by far is plastic laminate, such as Formica®. It is inexpensive, comes in a multitude of colors and patterns, and meets the standards mentioned above. As with any surface, however, plastic laminate will not stand up to rotary cutting. Use the specially designed rotary cutting mats only.

Painted or stained wood countertop is an alternative, but use caution. Wood and its finish is easily damaged from pins, scissors and other sharp objects. If you choose to use paint, use an oil-based paint because water-based paint responds more quickly to heat by getting sticky. Also, it takes 30 days for paint to cure totally. Do not use the countertop heavily during that time.

Other surfaces include hardwood, tile, and solid surfaces such as Corian®. These may not be the best choice for one or more of the following reasons: cold, uneven, hard to clean, easily damaged with pins or heat, or expensive.

WINDOWS

Natural light is important for a sewing space. Its main importance is psychological. Not much beats sewing in a sun-filled space. A sewing space with natural light also helps with efficiency when trying to blend or match threads and fabric.

With a window comes a need to create window treatments. There are two types of window treatments: privacy and decorative. A popular method of providing privacy is with the use of mini, micro-mini, or honeycomb (Duette) blinds. These treatments raise and lower easily while taking up very little space within the window and are widely available.

The privacy blind must be treated as if it were wall space and must provide high light reflectance. You need a privacy blind even if privacy is not a factor. Without a light-colored blind covering the window at night, the light literally flies out the window! Don't believe it? Try it! Leave the windows bare one night, then cover with a white sheet. You'll be amazed at the difference in the room's lighting.

There are an infinite number of ideas for decorative window treatments. Have fun with this part of your decor! See *Creative Serging for the Home and Other Quick Decorating Ideas* for ideas and how-tos.

Countertop edges can vary in design. Below are examples of a 45° beveled edge, a wood trim edge, a rounded edge, and a 90° edge.

CEILING AND WALLS

The ceiling and wall surface should provide high light reflectance (see page 52) so the keep the colors light. The walls are also used as backdrops for organizational systems, cabinets and art, so keep them plain and neutral in color.

Paint

Paint is the least expensive and the simplest wall treatment. Consider adding a little interest with rag or sponge painting, stenciling, or painting a mural or graphic for a focal point. These decorative ideas are especially appropriate in a sewing professional's client reception area (see page 105).

Wallpaper

Wallpaper adds interest to the room and can hide some wall inconsistencies that paint tends to highlight. Your choice should be a subtle pattern, color or texture, with extra interest added by a border. Remember, there is a lot of activity in the sewing space. Try to keep visual busyness to a minimum.

Fabric

Fabric on one or more walls may be a fun choice, especially for a client reception area. Try starching the fabric directly to the walls following Judy Lindahl's directions in *Decorating with Fabric* (see page 127). Or, create an upholstered look. Consider using Quik Trak to hang a piece of your favorite fabric to enjoy until the time is right to sew it. Quik Trak is also a great choice for camouflaging basement walls! Quik Trak is simply a plastic channel track that does not damage the fabric. Change the fabric for a new enjoyment pleasure. Change the fabric with the seasons or with the holidays. The fabric becomes a focal point in your space—like a piece of art.

Note: See *Creative Serging for the Home and Other Quick Decorating Ideas* for photos of rooms featuring starched fabric and Quik Trak. To see Quik Trak in action, view the video, *Creative Home Decorating* (see pages 127-128).

Color, Line and Design

When planning the layout, design and colors, it is important to keep some basic truths in mind.

- White accents reflect light and help visually enlarge a room. They lend an airy, spacious feeling.

- Soft shades of yellow visually enlarge a room. If you add white, this normally warm color takes on a cooler tone.

- Tints of blue and white create an open look that's also relaxing and comforting.

- Neutral colors tend to create a spacious feeling because they recede—making walls look farther away than they actually are. To "liven-up" neutral colors, add visual interest with texture—sponge paint the walls! Also consider adding accents in a bold color.

- To visually eliminate angles from a sloped ceiling, paint the wall color as far up as possible. This will help the room look taller than it actually is.

- Moldings and trim should be similar in color to their surroundings so they don't break up the space unnecessarily. Paint the baseboards to reflect the floor color; door and window molding to reflect the wall color.

- Simple window treatments soften the break a window makes in a wall.

- Vertical lines draw the eye up and seemingly raise the ceiling. You can use wallpaper with narrow stripes in a soft pastel color and white to create the tallest but least obtrusive effect.

- Small, narrow spaces, such as hallways, should be painted in pale colors and lit with overhead lights. This will make them appear more spacious.

Wall Systems & Dividers

Wall Organizers

Using your walls to their fullest potential while keeping them enjoyable to look at is an interesting challenge. Here are some wall-organizing ideas.

Pegboard

Good old-fashioned pegboard is still a practical option in a sewing space. The versatility of pegboard is hard to beat. It can be used to store just about everything. There are several hook and storage systems designed for pegboard. Hardware stores have the standard choices and mail-order hardware catalogs have more (see resource section). See pages 15 and 34 for pegboard in action! Consider painting it a pleasing color or try a different paint technique such as sponge painting or splatter painting to liven it up.

Note: When mounting pegboard to a wall, use spacers to give a little "wiggle" room for slipping the hooks into the board.

Grid Systems

A contemporary version of pegboard is a vinyl-coated grid system. It can incorporate a variety of hooks, baskets, clips and racks to be inserted into the wall-hung gridded panel. See page 66 for a grid system in action.

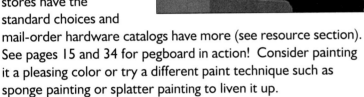

Slatwall

A more unusual wall system is the "slatwall" used by many retailers and available through display houses (see resource section). Many various baskets, hooks, shelves, brackets, and displayers slip into the slots. The ideas are limitless!

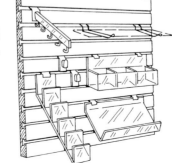

Bulletin Boards

Some form of bulletin board is a necessity in the sewing space. It can be used to hang guidesheets and pattern tissues of projects in progress (it's a Murphy's Law that you will need that tissue as soon as you fold it up and put it away, so fool Murphy and don't put it away until the project is complete!), notes about a project, lists of projects in progress and ideas of future projects. You may even want to pin up pictures of your loved ones so when you are finishing that Easter dress at 2 a.m. you'll remember why you're doing it.

If you can fit in only one bulletin board, locate it near the sewing machine for pinning up the guidesheet. This way you only have to look up to see what the next step is. Hang a pencil or pen on a ribbon and check off each step when done.

Homosote and other rigid Styrofoam insulation are optional products you can use for a bulletin board. Available from home improvement stores, they come in various size sheets. Cover them with fabric.

Wesystems has a product designed to display paper products that works well in the sewing space. It grips paper with friction gripping rollers so it does not damage the paper (see resource section, page 122).

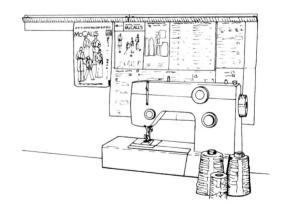

Room Dividers

Many sewing spaces share a larger room with other family activities. Room dividers may be a nice addition to the space. They can serve many purposes—adding needed wall space, acting as a visual divider, adding privacy for fitting, acting as a reminder to family members that this space is yours...or serving as a temporary wall to hide the "project in progress" from unexpected company.

♦ Use bookcases facing into the rest of the room. Cover the back with corkboard to create a bulletin board for the sewing space, or hang a gridded wall panel, slot wall panel or pegboard from the back to become a storage wall for the sewing space.

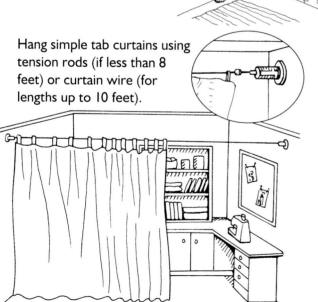

Or face the shelves into the sewing area for storage and cover the back with decorator fabric or maps or posters or...the possibilities are limitless!

Hang simple tab curtains using tension rods (if less than 8 feet) or curtain wire (for lengths up to 10 feet).

♦ Use a free-standing grid system as a divider. The back could be draped with fabric if you don't want to be able to see into the system.

Folding Screens

Folding screens can also be used as room dividers and have the added plus of being lightweight and easy to move and store if needed. For stability, folding screens need to be built as three sections hinged together. There are many, many ways to create folding screens, including the following:

♦ **Pocket Screens...**like big pillowcases with fabric hinges sewn in to create pockets for foam-core. Since these can be pinned into, use them as portable bulletin boards! Using the full width of two decorator or fashion fabrics (54-60" wide and 2 1/2 to 3 yards in length). Stitch the two fabrics right sides together using a 1/4" seam allowance and leaving one short side open. Trim, clip and turn right side out. Press well, and press under 1/4" on the open side. Divide the finished width measurement by 3. Draw a line that dimension in from each side. (e.g. if the finished measurement is 53", draw a line 17 2/3" from each finished side which creates three sections 17 2/3" wide.) Double-needle topstitch on the lines, creating the hinges for the screen. Then slip in 1/2" foam-core or rigid insulation into the pockets you just created. Hand stitch the opening closed.

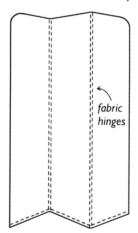

fabric hinges

Leave open at bottom to insert foam-core, then hand stitch closed.

Note: Foam-core is available at art-supply stores and comes in various sizes up to 4'x8' sheets. Know your needed dimensions and have the store cut the sheets for you. If they cannot cut them, use an X-Acto® knife and a metal straight edge to score the right side then the back, and it'll cut apart. Homosote and other rigid insulation are available from home remodeling stores.

♦ Use a pegboard system for one side of a framed folding screen and corkboard for the other for a storage and idea wall all in one.

♦ Use a pegboard system on one side and fabric on the other if the folding screen needs to be pretty from one side.

## CHAPTER 5

LIGHTING AND ELECTRICAL

Lighting is a part of your environment. It affects the mood, color, safety, convenience and decorative quality of your space. In addition, poor posture and poor lighting are the two major reasons for human fatigue. Too much or too little light can make you feel tired. Therefore, it's important to learn a bit about lighting, starting with some common lighting terms.

Contrary to popular belief, **wattage** doesn't indicate how much light will be given. It is the electrical measurement of input to the light source. Wattage is the measurement of how much energy is used. **Lumens** are the units measuring light quantity produced by a light source. They are the actual lighting output.

Note: Lumens and wattage are listed on a bulb's sleeve.

As a rule of thumb, the most visually demanding tasks require a total of at least 2500 lumens (150 watt bulb). A casual demand on the eyes, such as watching television requires only 1500-2000 lumens (100 watt bulb).

Footcandles indicate the amount of lumens that actually reach the surface where the light is needed. **Foot lamberts** are the amount of light that is reflected off the surface and reaches the eyes.

Consider three main factors when developing the lighting plan for your sewing space:

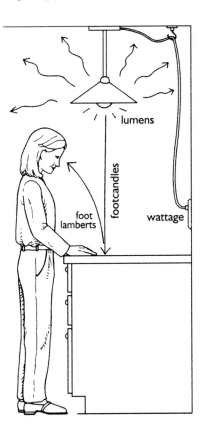

1. The reflectance levels of all major surfaces.

2. The types of lighting.

3. The differences among incandescent, fluorescent and halogen lights.

LIGHT REFLECTANCE

The amount of light reflected from the surfaces being illuminated affects the total amount of light needed. The lighter the surface, the more reflection and the less lighting required. The darker the surface, the less reflectance and more lighting required. Shiny, smooth surfaces reflect more light than dull, textured ones; however, be aware that shiny, smooth surfaces coupled with bright light can create uncomfortable glare.

Know that the reflected light will be tinted by the color of the reflecting surface. Light striking a warm yellow surface will reflect a warm yellow color, while light striking white walls, ceiling and counters will reflect a clean white color.

The following are average reflectance levels for the surfaces in your space:

Ceiling	60% - 90%
Walls	35% - 60%
Floors	15% - 35%
Countertops	30% - 50%

TYPES OF LIGHTING

For sewing spaces and indeed for most work environments, high reflectance colors are desirable for walls and ceilings to provide good light bounce-off. Moderate reflectance is desired for counter surfaces because this will give good light without a risk of glare, and lower reflectance levels are acceptable on cabinet finishes and flooring.

A good lighting plan utilizes three types of artificial lighting as well as natural light to achieve the best illumination. The artificial lighting includes ambient (general), accent (mood) and task lighting. For a sewing space, we are primarily concerned with general and task lighting. However, professional dressmakers may want to include accent lighting in the client reception area.

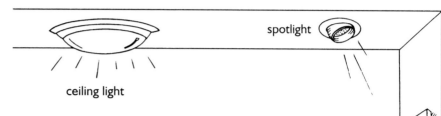

spotlight

ceiling light

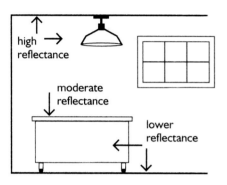

high → reflectance

moderate reflectance

lower reflectance

Use the following chart to help with your color decisions about light reflectance:

Color	% of light reflected
White	85
Light Colors	
Cream	75
Gray	75
Yellow	75
Buff	70
Green	65
Blue	55
Medium Colors	
Yellow	65
Buff	63
Gray	55
Green	52
Blue	35
Dark Colors	
Gray	30
Red	13
Brown	10
Blue	8
Green	7
Wood Finishes	
Maple	42
Satinwood	34
English Oak	17
Walnut	16
Mahogany	12

Ambient Lighting

Ambient or general lighting is the foundation of a lighting plan and provides the room with overall illumination. It should be a comfortable level of illumination that allows you to see and perform general activities. In most cases try to incorporate at least two sources of central, bright, well-diffused, and evenly spaced light. This is usually accomplished with ceiling-mounted light fixtures. The goal of ambient lighting is to make sure all open spaces are free of annoying shadows, so the greater the room's dimensions the more light sources are needed.

Mood Lighting

Mood or accent lighting can create a dramatic welcome to your friends, family and clients. Consider highlighting an architectural feature, art object, plant, a furniture grouping, or a beautiful piece of fabric!

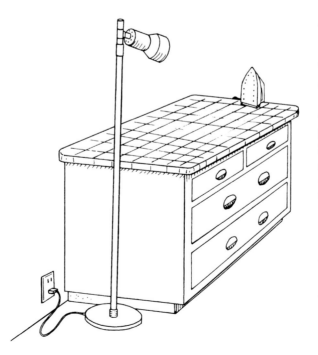

Task Lighting

Task lighting must occur wherever a work activity is taking place, such as the sewing center, the cutting center, the pressing center and the fit center. It should be glare-free and shadowless to help prevent tired eyes and fatigue. Task light directs a pool of illumination on areas where vision will be concentrated. Of the 2500 lumens required for a visually demanding task, the greatest number of lumens should be concentrated in task lighting.

LIGHTING SOURCES

There are four sources from which modern light comes. Three sources are artificial: incandescent, halogen and fluorescent; and one is natural: sunlight.

Natural Light

Natural light enters the room through windows and/or skylights. Depending on their orientation, the time of day, the season and the weather, natural light can have either a harsh or gentle effect on the room. It is not a constant light and must be accompanied with artificial sources.

Incandescent

An **incandescent** lamp (filament lamp or light bulb) produces light by a filament heated by the flow of electric current through it. The filament is usually of tungsten wire and operated in the range of 4,000° F. Incandescent lamps come in many sizes, wattages and shapes, and in clear, frosted or white-coated bulbs. They are available in many special types for particular applications.

Incandescent lighting is the most common form of lighting and is found in most homes. You may have an existing ceiling surface-mount incandescent fixture in your sewing space now. It provides a natural, soft, warm, reddish cast that is flattering to people and intensifies warm colors. The warm part can be literal also, because incandescent fixtures give off heat. In incandescent bulbs, the tungsten wire is heated to around 4,000° F. The brighter the lamp, the higher the temperatures and the shorter the life of the lamp. Lamps generally offer 750-1,000 hours of lamp life. Extended-life lamps may offer 2,500 hours of operation, but they put out 20% less light.

The correct lamp is an important part of the incandescent lighting plan. An A-lamp or general-service lamp is a common household light bulb. Because of its multi-directional distribution of light, it's used in surface-mounted or suspended fixtures. Recessed and enclosed fixtures use R-lamps (reflector lamps) where the beam of light is directed outward and downward by a mirror-like reflective surface inside. Thus the throw of light can be controlled. Both spotlights and floodlights are available. The difference is in the width of the beam, which depends on the density of the frosting on the inside of the lamp.

Halogen

Halogen bulbs are about the size of a fountain-pen cap and can produce as much light as a standard incandescent bulb ten times their size. They also use about half the power while lasting up to seven times longer. Halogen is a rich, blue-white color that comes closer than any other artificial source to duplicating the color spectrum of sunlight.

Halogen (quartz) lighting has its filament in a quartz enclosure filled with halogen gas. Due to a regenerative cycle, the evaporated tungsten is removed from the bulb wall and redeposited on the filament. As a result, lamp blackening is eliminated and lamp life is roughly double standard incandescent lamps.

Halogen bulbs also produce twice the heat. (Halogen energy is even used in smooth-top cooking units.) They must be used with porcelain sockets only because most plastic ones cannot handle the intense heat. Keep this heat in mind because it may affect wall surfaces if used in sconces. Halogens can also fade surfaces. Place them at least 12" from the side wall, art or any fabric, dried flowers, etc. Double check before using a halogen bulb to replace an incandescent bulb. It is best to use these bulbs with fixtures designed for them.

Extra care must be taken to keep halogen lamps clean and scratch-free. Even the oil in your skin can create a point of weakness in the quartz tube and could cause it to break prematurely, rupturing at the point of contact when the lamp is turned on. Wear gloves or use a soft cloth when changing the bulb. If you touch it, clean it with rubbing alcohol. As a side note, do not plug the receiver for a cordless phone into the same outlet as a halogen lamp—the phone will buzz.

Fluorescent

A **fluorescent** lamp produces light by the excitation of phosphors, which emit light when subjected to ultraviolet radiation. The radiation results from an electric discharge caused by the flow of current through a metallic vapor or gas (usually a combination of mercury and argon). The phosphors form a coating on the inside of the fluorescent tube, surrounding the electric discharge. Fluorescent lamps come in varying colors, diameters, lengths and wattages. Fluorescent lights may be your best choice, and may actually soon be required by law. They use 60% less energy than standard incandescent bulbs. Most fluorescent lamps provide 7,500-10,000 hours of light. Fluorescent fixtures have come a long way in recent time, with manufacturers offering fine, close-to-the-ceiling fixtures that rival incandescent in quality and design. Today's fluorescents rely on electronically upgraded rapid-start bulbs that rarely flicker. These new bulbs also have a phosphorous coating inside the glass that renders colors far better than earlier models. In fact, on the lighting designer's color rendition index (CRI), some of the new fluorescent lamps are achieving admirable scores—a few as high as 80 or more on the CRI scale of 1 to 100, with 100 the truest. (Halogen lamps approach a perfect 100.)

When purchasing a fluorescent fixture, check the ballast rating; the ballast causes the buzzing. An "A" rating is the quietest and the best.

The tube choice is another important decision. The "deluxe warm white" fluorescent tube is best used when combining with incandescent lighting because it has the same reddish cast. The "deluxe cool white" should be used when a true color rendition is wanted. The "full spectrum" or "color corrected" tubes closely duplicate natural light.

Compact fluorescent light bulbs can screw into regular incandescent sockets and are manufactured to replace the incandescent bulb. A desk or floor lamp with a compact fluorescent bulb will not cast a shadow like that of a lamp with an incandescent bulb. When shopping for fluorescent, check total lumens rather than wattage. Remember, lumens measure total light output. (See chart on page 52.) The price is considerably higher than incandescent at the original investment, but the long-term value is well worth the initial expense.

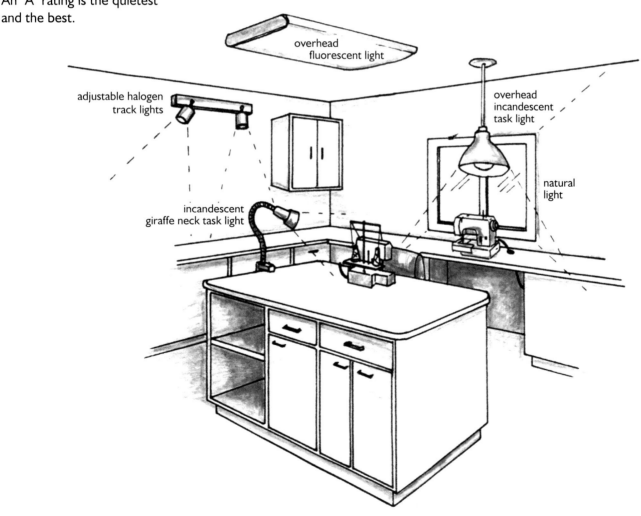

overhead fluorescent light

adjustable halogen track lights

overhead incandescent task light

natural light

incandescent giraffe neck task light

LIGHTING PLAN

Where do we place the chosen lights? Let's take a look.

Ambient Light

The purpose of overhead lights is to illuminate the entire room without shadows or glare. To ensure an even spread of light, locate all fixtures based on light beam spread information available from the manufacture.

Consider using halogen for recessed down lighting or track lighting. Using halogen allows for more light with fewer light heads, making these fixtures feasible. Also, consider recessed compact fluorescent fixtures. They are similar in appearance to the incandescent, but the light will be whiter. These fixtures also have a wide beam spread and give off as much light as a 150 watt incandescent thereby decreasing the number of fixtures needed.

Track lighting offers great versatility because the individual lights can be moved and angled to point in any direction. However, many heads are needed on the track to get good overall light. The more heads, the more heat.

As mentioned earlier, the best choice for lighting may be fluorescent ceiling-mount fixtures. Space these fixtures at **even** intervals in your room.

If your sewing space currently has only one ceiling light centered in the room and you need more, it is not difficult or cost prohibitive to add more. If you have an open attic area above your space, you may be able to "pigtail" electricity off the existing light to add others. If the current light location cannot be used, cover the existing electrical box with a metal plate. Once it is painted to match the ceiling, it blends in well. If an attic space is not above the room, the addition of lights is still possible without costly wallboard work. Pigtailing off the existing light can still be done, but the wires run on the ceiling surface, then must be covered with a special channel called exterior conduit. Again, once the conduit is painted to match the ceiling, it is unobtrusive.

If your space is quite large, consider switching sections of lights independently of each other. Perhaps you are only going to use the planning area and do not need the whole room lit. Also, consider putting the lights on a dimmer switch. This will allow you total control over the light output.

Task Lighting

To ensure adequate light for every task, every work area needs to have task lighting. Task lighting sources can be recessed, under-the-counter, track, chain-hung, or table or floor lamps.

The best light for close work like sewing comes from behind and over the shoulder. Unfortunately many times this is not feasible. A floor lamp would be the simplest way to accomplish this, but it tends to get in the way during the normal shift-and-scoot routine of sewing. The space may be designed so no activity is occurring to the left of each work station thus eliminating the need to shift the chair in that direction. Perhaps at least one of the work stations may be placed with a wall behind it allowing the mounting of a track light to shine over the shoulder. Reality dictates, at least for most of us, the need to mount a task light in front of or to the side of the work area. One of the best and simplest task lights is a swing-arm desk lamp. Try to mount the lamp to the countertop to eliminate the need for a base.

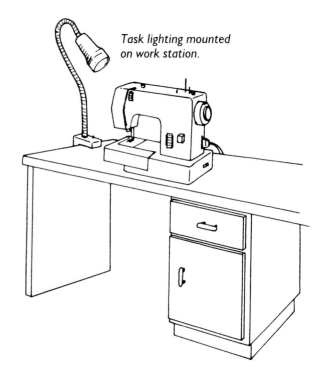

Task lighting mounted on work station.

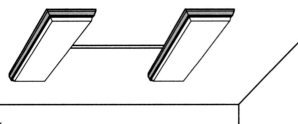

Another idea is to mount track lights to the wall or ceiling above the work station. These lights can be adjusted to where the beam of light is needed.

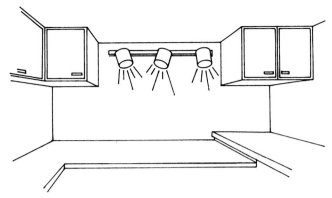

Studies show that for optimum light a hanging light should be mounted 15" to 18" above the work surface, 12" to 15" from the front of the counter and off to one side. However, at these heights the fixture would be in the way. Hang the light 24" to 30" above the work surface, and if necessary, use a higher output bulb.

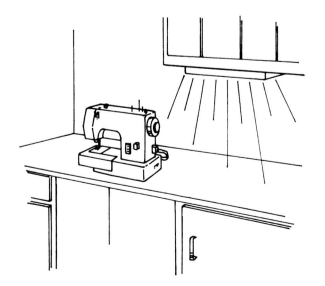

Fluorescent lights designed for installing under the wall cabinets in kitchens—called under-cabinet lights—can also be used in the sewing room as task lights.

If the lights are mounted to the ceiling, be sure to place them so your head will not cast a shadow on your work. For example, a track or recessed light placed above the sewing machines needs to be mounted 18" to 22" from the adjoining wall.

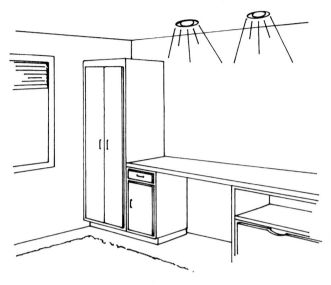

Note: Video screens and computer screens require low-level illumination to prevent glare. In fact, you may need to dim the overhead lights to decrease the glare in the eyes. Do not use fluorescent lighting as task lighting, and be attentive to the location of windows that can also cause glare (see page 111). When lighting the fitting area, avoid directing the light into the mirror.

Accent Lighting

To add drama or mood to your space, highlight a selected item or detail by using concentrated light (at least three times more light output than the general lighting around the subject area) focused on the subject. The lights most commonly used are recessed, adjustable spot lighting or low-voltage recessed lighting. The proper accent lighting can make a room look much larger than it actually is.

ELECTRICAL

You may live in an older home where electrical outlets and circuits are scarce. Sewing machines require very little electricity (about 100 watts), but heating equipment such as irons and a press require around 1,200 watts. A sewing room requires outlets—extension cords are a no-no. It is dangerous to have your machines, irons, TV, radio, etc. all plugged into one outlet. If this is the case, add additional outlets. Also, if you have too many items on a circuit, consider adding circuits. A standard circuit provides up to 1,500 watts of electricity safely. If, while you use the iron, the refrigerator comes on and the circuit trips or the fuse blows, you are overloaded on that circuit and an additional circuit must be added.

Adding electrical outlets and circuits is not impossible, even in an old house. However, it can be expensive especially if your sewing room is on the top floor and your electrical panel is in the basement. Often wire for the circuit can be encased in exterior conduit, run up the exterior of the house, brought into the house, then turned into outlets.

If your circuits are not overloaded, adding extra electrical outlets need not be expensive if you pigtail off an existing outlet and run the wiring along the baseboard, as mentioned with adding extra light sources. Wires must be covered with exterior conduit. Since sewing machines require very little energy, pigtailing is a workable option. If you simply need more plug-in spaces where there is an existing outlet, a multi-outlet power strip is considered safe. Choose one with a built-in circuit breaker to provide additional protection against overloading.

Irons and other pressing equipment, however, are another story and, if possible, should have a dedicated circuit. (Window air conditioners also use a lot of power. Never plug one into an outlet that shares a circuit with an iron.)

If you are building, dedicate three circuits to your sewing space—one for lights, one for the general outlet and one for the pressing equipment's outlet.

Consider putting the outlets on a switch. Then when you leave your studio, simply flip the switches and cut power to all your equipment!

Note: If you are doing any rewiring, be sure to contact a qualified electrician for advice. Any rewiring or new wiring must meet electrical code requirements and be approved by the local building inspector. If you're unsure of local electrical codes or your home's electrical system's capacity, contact a qualified electrician. Find out your circuit's capacity and the existing load and do not exceed the recommended capacity. Never overload the circuits!

Placement of Outlets

The best location for the outlets that service the sewing machines is behind the knee space. For instance, if the machines are along a wall, the outlet would be on the wall directly below the machines, not at the counter level. If the machine is on an island, the outlet would be mounted to the side of an adjoining cabinet. Excess cord on the counter is exposed to damage from pins, scissors, etc.

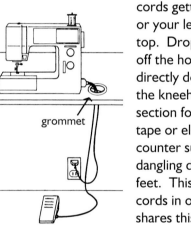

grommet

To eliminate the hassle of the machine cords getting wrapped up with the chair or your leg, drill a hole in the counter-top. Drop in a special grommet to finish off the hole, and run the machine's cord directly down from the machine and into the kneehole space. (See the resource section for grommet information.) Use tape or elastic and hook below the counter surface to keep cords from dangling down and fighting with your feet. This system will also help keep cords in order if more than one machine shares this space.

Note: If you have a computerized sewing machine, consider plugging your machine into a surge protector, which would save it from the possibility of de-programming in a power surge. All computers should be plugged into one.

Be sure to have power to all islands and to the end of peninsulas. Also, be aware of building codes on electricity. Codes will require an outlet every 6' of wall space regardless of whether you want one there or not. Electrical building codes prohibit the covering up of an outlet with built-in furniture. You must cut a hole in the back of the cabinet to allow access to the outlet.

## CHAPTER 6

PRIMARY & SECONDARY WORK CENTERS

Every sewing space must include the primary work centers...sewing, cutting and pressing, and storage. Secondary work centers need not be included in the sewing space itself, but should be available nearby. We have seen these centers in action on previous pages; now let's look at ways to create these centers.

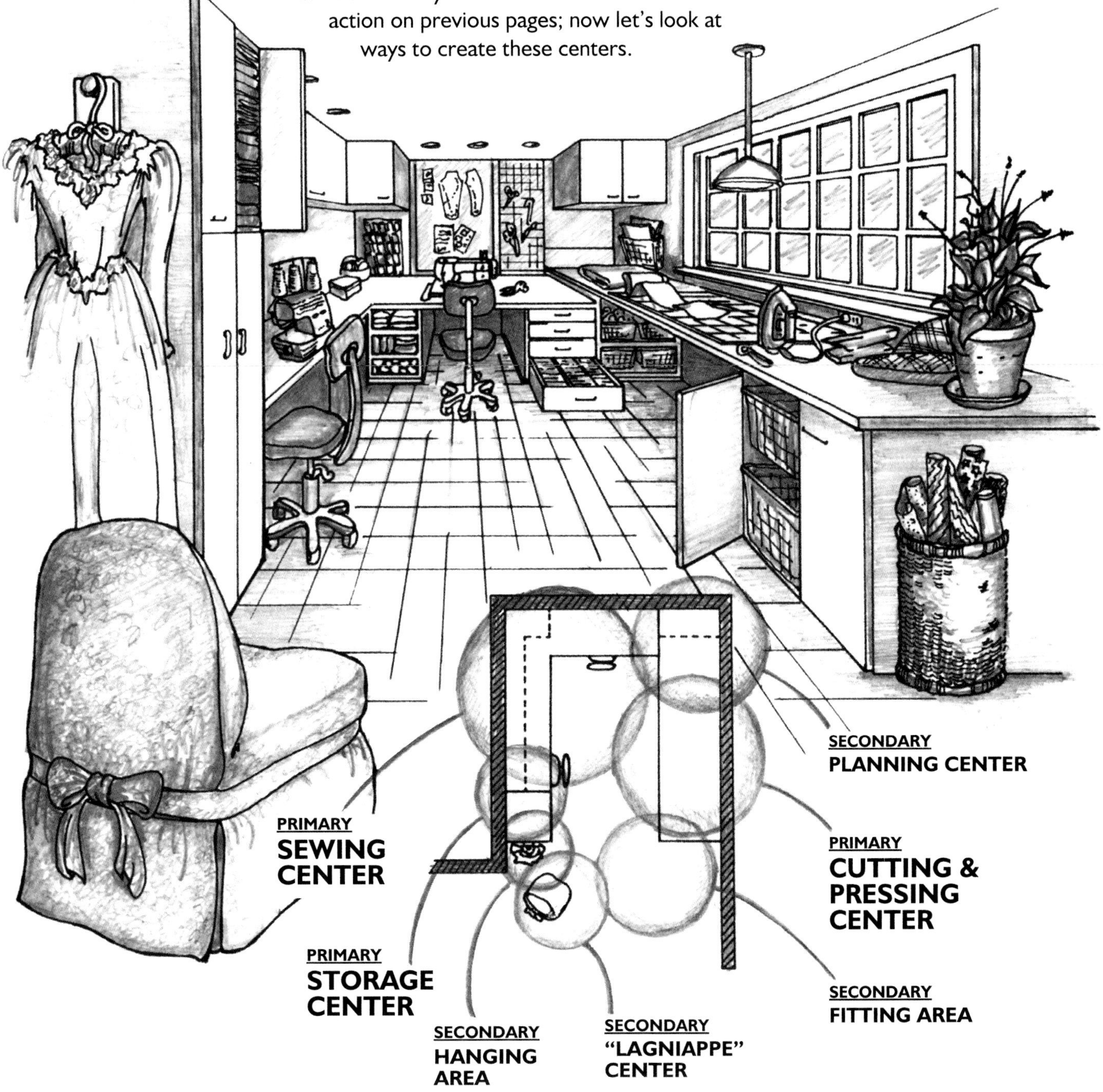

SECONDARY
PLANNING CENTER

PRIMARY
SEWING
CENTER

PRIMARY
CUTTING &
PRESSING
CENTER

PRIMARY
STORAGE
CENTER

SECONDARY
HANGING
AREA

SECONDARY
"LAGNIAPPE"
CENTER

SECONDARY
FITTING AREA

PRIMARY CENTERS

THE SEWING CENTER

The sewing center used to mean space for the sewing machine. Now, however, we have one or more sewing machines, sergers and maybe even embroidery machines! As mentioned before, for efficient sewing, a minimum of 24" of counter space is needed per machine.

- An inexpensive way to create a sewing center is to build only countertops and add storage under the counter with wire rolling-rack systems, wicker baskets, and boxes.

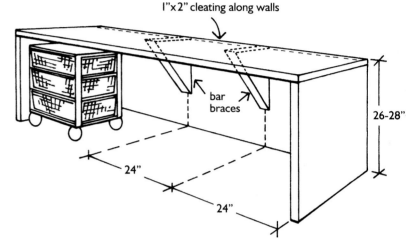

- Another inexpensive method of creating a sewing center is to use recycled kitchen or bath cabinets, dressers or filing cabinets. Spiff them up with a new coat of paint. This is a great place to try a new paint technique such as rag rolling, sponge painting or glazing. Then attach a countertop between the units for a sewing surface.

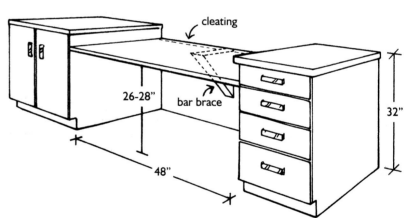

- Use bathroom cabinets. Cut 2" or 3" off the toe kick, cleat from the wall with a 2"x4" piece of wood, and for an extra 3" in depth, cover the entire area with a countertop.

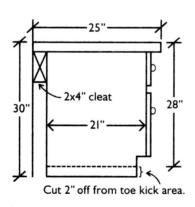

Cut 2" off from toe kick area.

Note: To ensure stability, a countertop must be supported every 2' with a bar brace or a leg brace (available from sewing mail-order catalogs or your local sewing or hardware store). If you must space farther than 4' without support, build a double-thickness countertop, which is two pieces of 3/4" pressboard rather than the standard one piece with a facia board. Support the counter-top along the wall using 1"x2" wood and on the free end, if there is one, use a solid panel.

In the previous examples the bed of the sewing machine is a couple of inches above the countertop. If you prefer the bed of your machine to be level with the countertop try the ideas on this page.

♦ Your local sewing machine store or sewing mail-order companies offer a Plexiglas extension made to fit your serger or sewing machine, creating a large flat surface. It can double as a light box if you place an 18" fluorescent light fixture under it. (See resource section.)

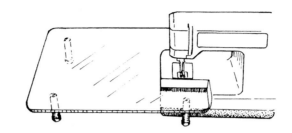

♦ Build a lowered platform just big enough for your machine, as shown here. You can use this technique when altering an old desk to fit your sewing machine. However, remember antiques lose their value if you change them in any way.

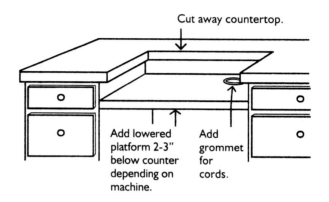

Cut away countertop.

Add lowered platform 2-3" below counter depending on machine.

Add grommet for cords.

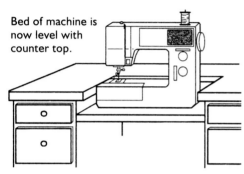

Bed of machine is now level with counter top.

Note: Parsons sells sewing machine inserts that will change your machine from a free arm to a flatbed. If you choose to use the insert, plan the opening to be 19 3/16" x 10 7/16", with curved corners to match the curves of the insert.

TIP: Attach adhesive-backed velcro dots to small, frequently used items and a velcro square to the front or top of your machine.

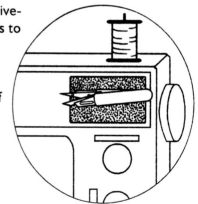

♦ Use two or three existing chests of drawers of the proper work height. Attach a platform between each and create a countertop to combine all.

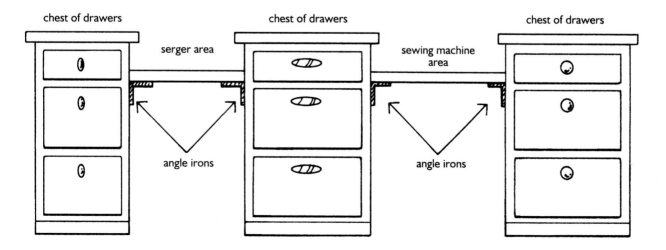

chest of drawers   chest of drawers   chest of drawers

serger area   sewing machine area

angle irons   angle irons

THE CUTTING AND PRESSING CENTER

♦ A great cut/press area can be created by using kitchen cabinets to build an island. In the kitchen, island cabinets normally house a cook top or sink, so they are screwed to the floor. But in the sewing space, the cabinets need not be secured in place. You can create any size island just by combining different-sized cabinets. The minimum size for a cut/press center is 30"x 36"; preferable size is at least 32"x 48" and up to as large as 48"x 84" (the size of a sheet of plywood or pressboard).

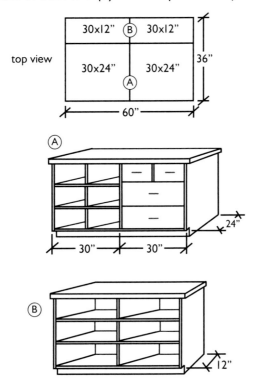

♦ Consider using old file cabinets, again jazzed up with a coat of paint. Raise a padded cut 'n' press board to the proper height with lumber or bricks. The finished height will be 35 1/4".

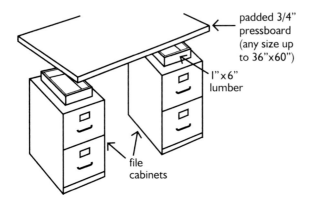

♦ Use an old structurally sound dresser, spruce it up with paint and make a cut 'n' press board (see page 64) to place on top.

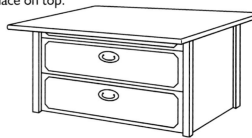

Note: If the drawers don't slide well, rub a bar of soap or beeswax on the area where the wood meets wood.

♦ Use spruced-up dressers or book shelves to support a flat paneled door (make sure the door is at least 32" wide). You may want to pad and cover the door or paint it. Raise height if necessary, as shown below.

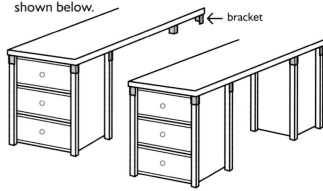

♦ Raise the height of an old dinette or banquet table and top with a padded cut 'n' press board.

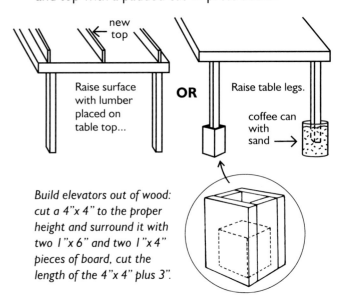

Build elevators out of wood: cut a 4"x 4" to the proper height and surround it with two 1"x 6" and two 1"x 4" pieces of board, cut the length of the 4"x 4" plus 3".

♦ Use the wall to store a cut/press area out of the way when not in use. Use plywood or a solid-core door and attach with a hinge to the wall. Don't use pressboard—it would be too heavy to lift.

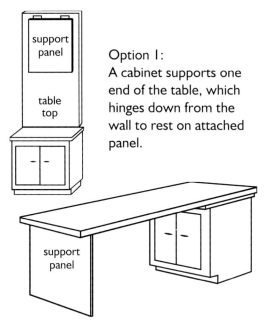

Option 1:
A cabinet supports one end of the table, which hinges down from the wall to rest on attached panel.

Option 2: Build a double-fold table with folding legs.

Note: Pre-made units are available from your local home builder's store or through specialty mail-order catalogs (see resource section).

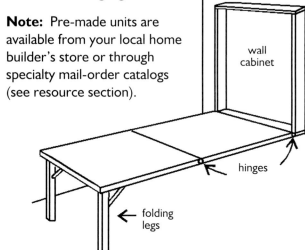

♦ Use two ironing boards set at the same height and lay a hollow-core door on them. (Again, you may choose to pad the door.) When not in use, store the door (perhaps behind a door) and fold up the ironing boards.

♦ Many cabinet companies offer great cutting tables. Some fold down for easy storage. In their smallest state they measure about 16"x40", with one leaf up they are 47"x40", and with both leaves up they are 72"x40". Many have built-in drawers and a shelf. (See resource section.)

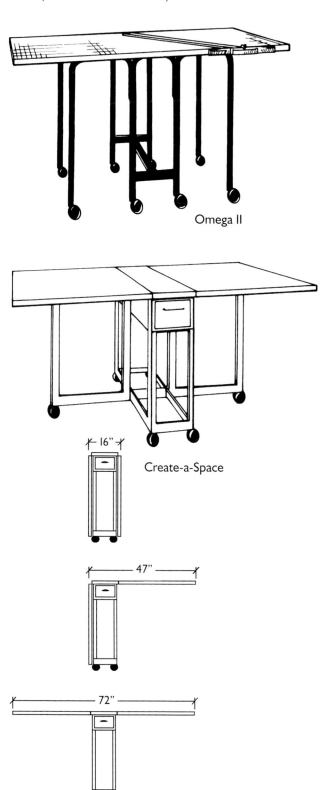

Omega II

Create-a-Space

MAKE A CUT 'N' PRESS BOARD

This large surface is a must! You can steam-shrink and cut fabric on it, and fuse interfacings on it.

fabric

pad

board

3. Starting in the center of one long side, wrap the padding to the back of the board and staple with a staple gun.

4. Finish one long side, then do the other long side, then the short ends, pulling the padding taut with each staple.

5. Trim away some of the padding to reduce the bulk on the corners.

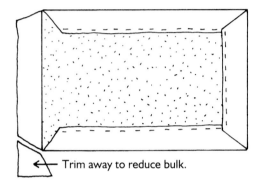

Trim away to reduce bulk.

6. Repeat procedure with the fabric chosen for the covering. You may choose to cover the staples with duct tape to prevent the staples from scratching you or your table.

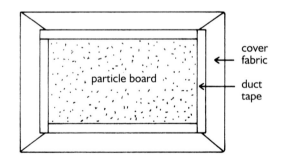

particle board

cover fabric

duct tape

To make a cut 'n' press board you will need:

♦ 1/2"-5/8" thick particle board (plywood can warp).

♦ 1/2" thickness of absorbent padding (old wool army blankets, 100% wool fabric or 100% cotton waffle cloth covered with heavy 100% cotton flannel.) (See resource section.)

♦ A cover of smooth muslin, medium-colored 1/4" checked gingham fabric, or blocking cloth.

1. Lay the padding on a flat surface.

2. Place the pressboard on top of it

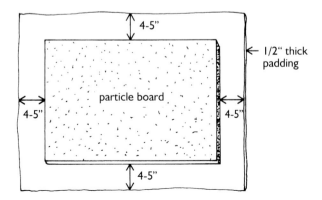

4-5"

1/2" thick padding

particle board

4-5"

4-5"

4-5"

The Spaceboard

As an alternative to the cut 'n' press board, a great addition to any cutting table, especially the fold-down models, is the Spaceboard created by Voster Marketing. This lightly padded board has a work surface of 33" x 51" and can fold in half for easy storage. You can press, steam, fuse, measure, pin, block and lay out on the board because of the way they are constructed. The top layer of fabric is a 100% cotton gridded fabric with a water-resistant lining and the bottom layer is covered with a black polyester felt-like fabric to prevent damage to the surface you are placing it on. (See resource section, page 122.)

Other Pressing Options

If your cut/press center is not a constant feature in your sewing space, then an additional smaller area that is always available must be planned. Let's look at space-saving ways this can occur.

♦ The good old-fashioned ironing board is necessary for some ironing tasks and lends itself to many sewing tasks as well.

Note: A new ironing board called the Shirt Master is available. Specially designed for pressing, it has a wider surface area and a more pointed end section. Great for sewing!

♦ Many ironing board systems that mount to the wall or pull out of a drawer are available from builders' hardware stores.

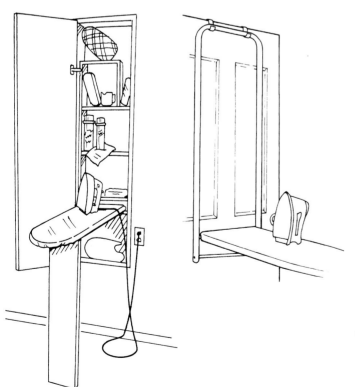

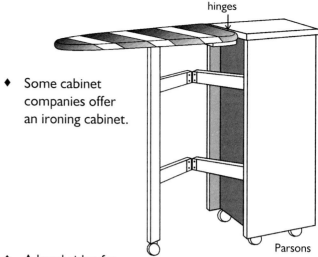

♦ Some cabinet companies offer an ironing cabinet.

Parsons

♦ A handy idea for a small localized pressing area is to place a small, portable cut 'n' press board on the edges of an open drawer.

The Press

An additional piece of pressing equipment is the press. You normally use this in a standing position, so it should be located at a comfortable height. In general, the press is not used as a primary press station, but you may want to locate it in or near your pressing area. Presses are lightweight and portable, so they are simple to store and set up when needed. If you use yours a lot, leave it set up and create a special center for it.

THE STORAGE CENTER

The storage area will be discussed in Chapter 6, so turn the page to look at secondary centers now.

SECONDARY CENTERS

THE HANGING AREA

A hanging area is important primarily for partially completed projects. You have pressed as you've sewn so you do not want to wad up the project and stuff it in a basket! Hang it on a hanger instead. Use the hanging space for:

♦ Storage of fabric (see page 72).

♦ Storage of planned projects waiting to be sewn. Hang the fabric on a hanger, place the pattern, notions and all findings in a Ziploc® bag. Punch a hole in the bag and slip it over the hanger. The project is ready to go when you are!

♦ Partially completed items with findings stored in the Ziploc bag.

♦ Projects completed up to the finishing. Buttons, thread, needle, and other hand-sewing items are in the bag ready for the phone to ring...stitch on buttons while talking on the phone!

♦ Completed projects waiting for delivery or pickup or for wrapping as gifts.

♦ Client projects waiting for a fitting or pickup.

♦ Projects waiting for altering or mending (ugh).

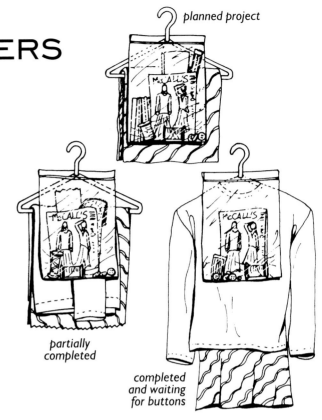

planned project

partially completed

completed and waiting for buttons

Kathleen Spike designed this grid unit for her sewing studio.

How To Create a Hanging Area

♦ Mount a clothes rod between wall cabinets or mount a wire shelf on the wall, 66" from the floor.

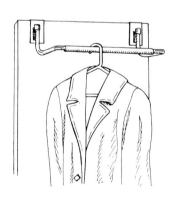

♦ Replace a door hinge pin with a special pin with hanging hooks available from a builder's hardware store or catalog.

♦ Attach to a wall, cabinet or door one of the many hanging rods, racks and poles available from hardware stores.

Note: Wreath hangers also work as over-the-door hanging hooks.

♦ Mount antique door handles or wooden pegs to a strip of wood and screw to the wall. Face it, we all use the door knobs to hang items, we might as well incorporate them into the design!

Note: To keep hangers from overlapping, mount the handles or pegs 24" apart.

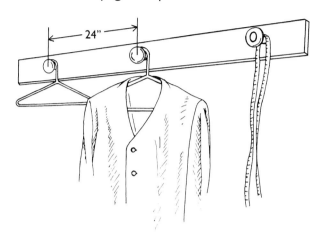

♦ Purchase one of the many commercial hanging racks available from a display house.

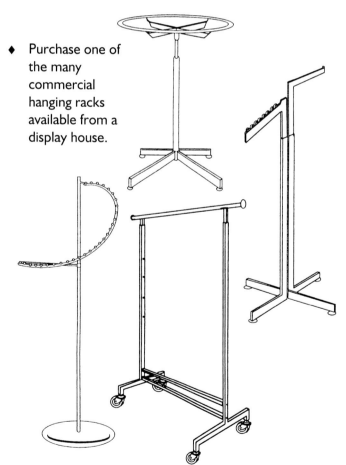

Catherine Stephenson

THE FITTING AREA

If you are a fashion-sewer, the sewing space should include at least a full-length mirror and a large hand-held mirror in the fitting area. However, if at all possible, include a three-way mirror to aid in fitting while you sew. The fitting area requires a minimum of a 4'x4' floor space.

Note: Mirrors should be a minimum size of 16" wide by 42" high. They should be placed with the top at 70" from the floor. Allow a 4'x5' minimum floor space in front of the mirror (4'x10' is better—then you can see all the way to your toes!).

♦ Here are ideas on how to build a three-way mirror to suit your needs.

♦ Here are ways to create a three-way image using the doors of a closet.

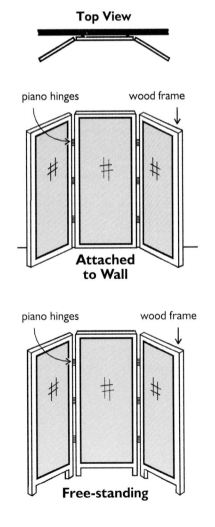

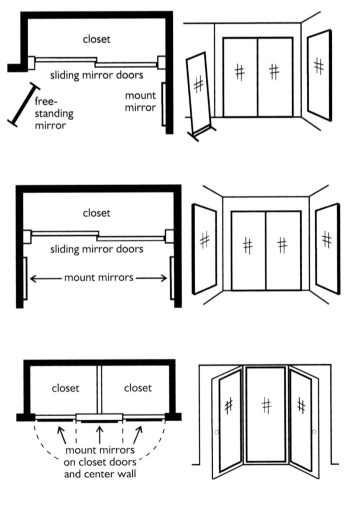

THE PLANNING CENTER

The planning center is the area where you stage projects you are planning to do as Marta Alto does here. (Not to be confused with the daydreaming area!) Let's say every year you sew up a storm creating a back-to-school wardrobe for your children. You purchase lots of fabric, patterns, thread and other findings for each project. The planning center is the area where you stage those projects, matching the pattern with the fabric, thread, etc. These individual piles may just remain as they are staged on the planning center or you may prefer to bag them in large Ziploc bags and store in wire baskets, plastic boxes, or whatever.

LAGNIAPPE CENTERS

lagniappe (lan yap'): A Creole word meaning a little something extra.
If you can possibly carve out the space, consider these additional areas when planning your sewing space:

Try to incorporate a TV/VCR unit into the sewing space. Many wonderful sewing videos are available and it is ideal to be able to watch them in the sewing room, ready to try out the techniques.

A comfortable chair, sofa or window seat with good light can be your area to do hand work comfortably, read the inspiring sewing and craft books and magazines now available, and daydream about ideas.

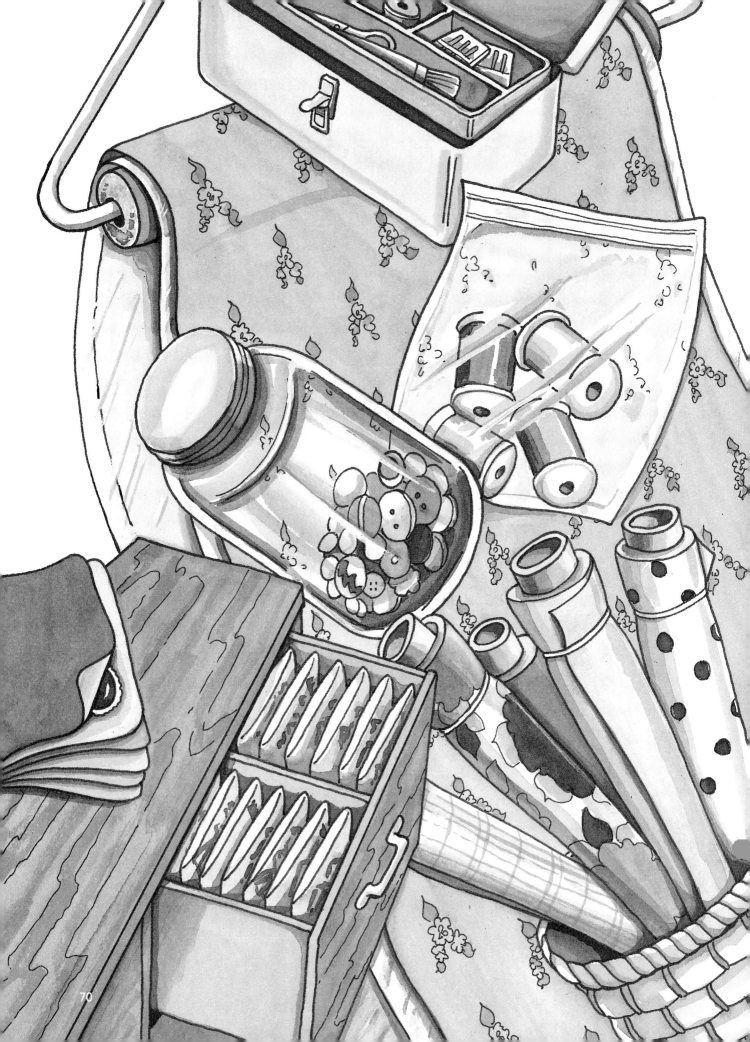

## CHAPTER 7

STORAGE AND ORGANIZATION

We've all heard the saying "she who dies with the most fabric wins." It's more than just fabric, it's a combination of all sewing "stuff." Let's look at options for all our important sewing items.

FABRIC

The Fabric Pantry

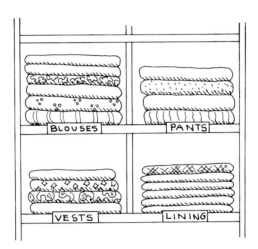

♦ Many dream kitchens incorporate a pantry and our dream sewing studio has a fabric pantry! The best depth for a fabric pantry is 18" (inside clearance would be about 16 fi"). This allows 60" wide fabric to be folded in quarters. Any narrower and the fabric gets folded too many times; deeper and small cuts get lost. Organize the fabric in the pantry according to color, fiber content and/or usage (e.g. linings would be separate from fashion fabric).

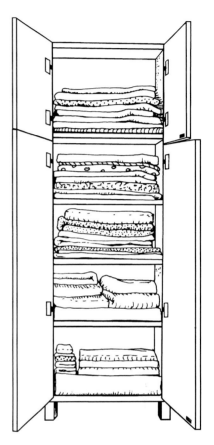

Further Organization

To further organize your fabric and thoughts, Joan and Karl Stoicheff of Sew Sensational have created a Fabriholics Treasure Chest. This 5fi"x8fi" inventory book allows you to staple fabric swatches to an inventory card on which you note the yardage, width, care, fiber content, date and location of purchase. Pattern inventory pages allow you to note the pattern company, number, size, yardage, designer, fabric recommended and notions needed. Also included are pages for button inventory where you note size, color, type, and date and location of purchase. All cards have space to staple or tape the fabric, button, copy or drawing of the pattern. (See resource section, page 121.)

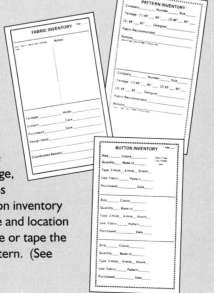

Note: Pin or staple a paper label to the selvage edge of each cut of fabric stating the fiber content, width, length, care instructions, and if it has been prewashed or preshrunk. This will save time later when the fabric has "aged to perfection" and can be used. Or, using a marker, note this information on the selvage.

Roll Fabric

Fine fabric, such as silks, wools and Ultrasuede® can be stored by rolling on recycled fabric tubes or bolts from the fabric store. When purchasing home-dec fabric, ask for the fabric to be rolled on a tube. This prevents wrinkles and folds.

Hang Fabric

Hang delicate fabric on a plastic hanger padded with hot-water-pipe foam insulation. Place an acid-free sheet of tissue paper over the foam, then hang the fabric.

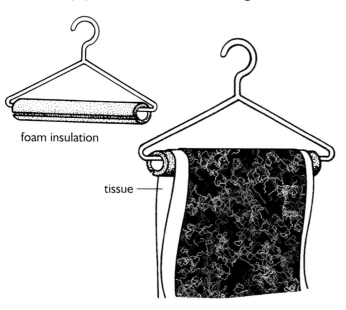

foam insulation

tissue

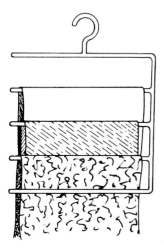

Skirt and pant hangers also work well.

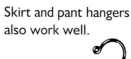

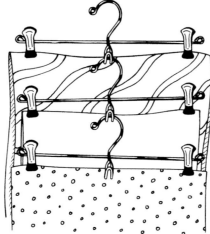

Make a storage caddy to hang from the ceiling or wall. Use sturdy fabric such as a decorator fabric. Fuse two pieces together for extra stability. Hang on a decorative dowel (from *Instant Interiors*, see resource page 122).

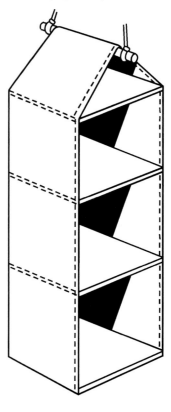

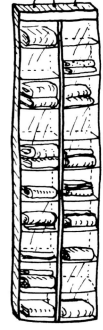

Hanging plastic sweater bags that zip shut also serve well for storing fabric.

Drawers

Drawers are a workable option for fabric storage. However, watch the depth of the drawer—digging is not a good use of energy!

Storage Boxes

Plastic

See-through plastic boxes such as Rubbermaid brand are an option. They come in many sizes and stack well. (Remember, for easy access, try not to stack more than two high.) Make sure the lid can be securely snapped on. Organize the contents of each box according to fiber content, color or usage as mentioned for the pantry on page 71. Also, label each box as to it's contents. A plastic recipe card sleeve can be taped to the box using double stick tape. This sleeve holds index cards. List the contents of the box and staple small fabric squares to them. As the contents change, edit the index card.

Note: If packed neatly these boxes can be visually appealing and add ambiance to the room. How many of us love to look at the bolts of quilting fabric stacked neatly in the store? Who wouldn't love to have a wall of fabric that looked just like that? Create that same effect with small cuts and remnants in see-through plastic boxes. However, be warned—textile experts say fabrics should not be stored in plastic bins or bags because they can cause yellowing of the fabric.

Cardboard

Cardboard boxes such as liquor boxes and file boxes are a great inexpensive option. They are heavy-duty cardboard and can be decorated with fabric, paint or contact paper. Since you cannot see inside the box, staple or tape squares of fabric with the yardage, width, and fiber content on the outside of the box. Also, preprinted, assemble-yourself boxes are available from variety stores and mail-order companies. They come in various sizes and shapes including under-the-bed storage boxes, file boxes, and chests of drawers.

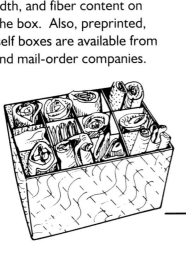

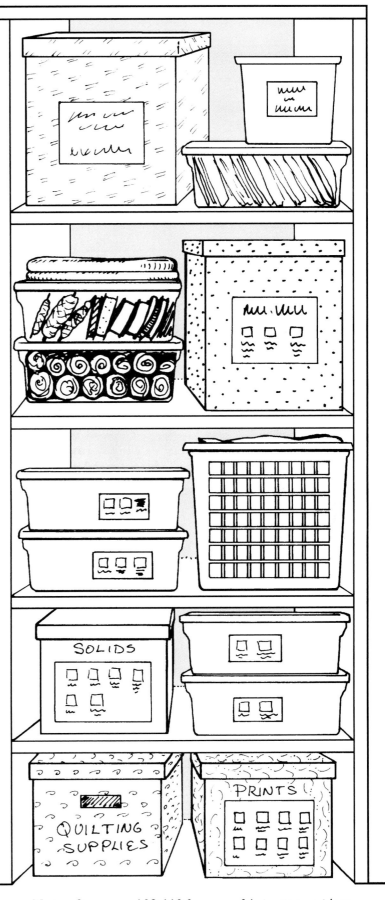

Note: See pages 109-110 for more fabric-storage ideas.

Fabric As Art

For that beautiful piece of tapestry, damask or silk that you just had to have, but haven't decided what to create yet, hang it on the wall to enjoy until you are ready to stitch it up. Install a curtain rod or wood dowel on the wall and drape the fabric over it. Or, use wooden quilt hangers, push pins or, for light weight fabric, the Piece Keeper by Blue Feather Products (see page 77).

Storing Interfacing

Lengths of interfacing should be stored on empty fabric bolts or wrapping paper tubes to prevent creasing. Use rubber bands to keep the interfacing from slipping off the tube and stuff the instructions including the brand name inside the tube.

Note: Store tubes upright in a basket, waste basket or sono tube. A sono tube is a concrete form and is available from a masonry supply store.

Use the printed plastic instruction sheets to make a bag for each brand and weight of interfacing. Fold the sheet in half and sew up the sides. Then slip the interfacing (and scraps) inside the bag. Store in a drawer, plastic bin or box.

Storing Trim

Wrap trims on empty paper towel and toilet paper tubes. Again hold in place with rubber bands or pins and store in appropriate-size boxes, bins or drawers.

Open packages of seam binding or rickrack can be kept tidy by slipping them into plastic recipe-saver sleeves, then stored in an appropriate-size box.

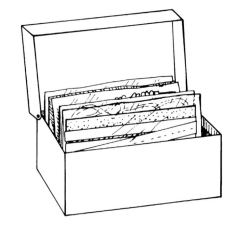

Patterns

Patterns seem to multiply in the night so plan to accommodate their exploding population!

Drawers & Cabinets

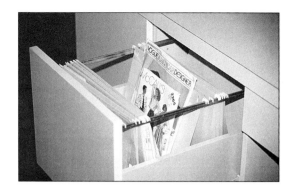

* **Drawers** are a wonderful choice for pattern storage. Consider installing dividers in the drawer to keep the patterns tidy. Dividers can be made with 1/8" hardboard cut to fit or have them installed by the cabinet company. (Drawer must be at least 9" deep on inside.)

  Note: The bottom two drawers of a standard three-drawer kitchen cabinet store patterns beautifully.

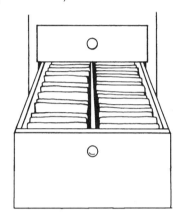

* **Office file cabinets** equipped with the hanging file system are a great way to store over-sized patterns or patterns with too many pieces to fit back into the pattern envelope! Repackage them into manila envelopes with the pattern envelope taped to the front. With this method you don't have to fight getting all the pieces back into the envelope.

  Note: After using a pattern, fold pieces and wrap all together in plastic wrap. They slide easily into the envelope and small pieces stay together.

  The file cabinet can also be used to file magazine articles, product and sewing machine instructions, pamphlets and other reference material.

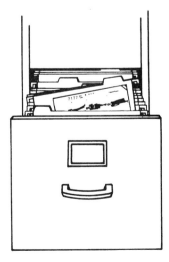

* **Wall cabinets** store patterns well. Adjust the shelves to store the **standard size** patterns on their sides. This allows the shelves to be placed closer together, giving more storage in the cabinet. Adjust one or two shelves farther apart so **larger patterns** can store upright.

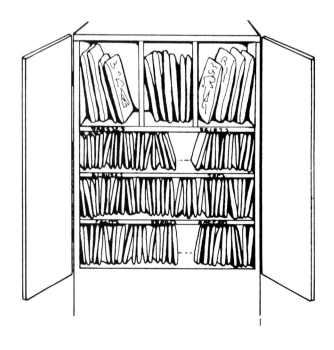

Boxes for Patterns

- **Cardboard** banker's boxes or file boxes available through variety and office-supply stores are also an option for pattern storage. The boxes can be stored on shelves, under countertops, or in closets. If they will be part of your decor, cover the boxes with fabric (see *Creative Serging for the Home and Other Quick Decorating Ideas* for the how-tos) or contact paper.

- Nancy's Notions sells a durable cardboard pattern box. It holds 30 patterns and features a handy index on the front of the box for recording pattern numbers, styles and sizes.

- **Shoe boxes**, without their lids, hold patterns in upright positions and keep the patterns tidy.

- **Tall, clear plastic sweater boxes** are also a great size for patterns.

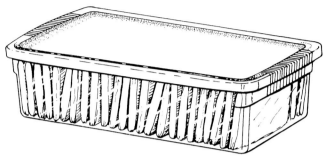

Hangers

Hang pieces of frequently used patterns over the bottom of clothes hangers. Pin through the pattern envelope and all layers of pattern pieces to hold in place. This saves wear and tear on the pattern and time spent trying to get the pattern back into the envelope.

Pattern Organization

♦ Photocopy the front and back cover of the pattern envelope. Punch holes and put in a three-ring binder with dividers indicating skirts, pants, tops, etc. You may consider going one step further and reducing the copy to fit into a small binder that will fit in your purse. File the actual patterns according to company and by number, just as the local fabric stores do. This method creates a cross-reference for you and makes patterns easy to find. If you have the same pattern in many different sizes, remember to note which sizes you have in your notebook. (See page 71 for information on a pre-made inventory book.)

Note: Custom dressmakers may choose to record patterns by the client.

♦ Another idea is to file the patterns by type, i.e. file all skirts together, pants together, jackets together, etc. If you are storing patterns in a divided drawer or in a wall cabinet, use colored markers to color code the end of the pattern, red for pants, blue for jackets, green for skirts, yellow for swimsuits, etc. Be sure to make yourself a note about what the codes stand for and tape it to the inside of the cabinet door or drawer.

Timesaving Tips

Do not refold and put the pattern tissues away until you have completed the project. It is a "Murphy's Law" of sewing that you will have to refer to a tissue piece after you have put it away. Using a large safety pin, pin the tissues and the pattern envelope together and hang on a cup hook or small nail. Or, place the tissue and envelope in a large Ziploc bag, punch a hole in the top and hang it on a cup hook or nail. Or if you have a large bulletin board or folding screen (see page 51), pin the tissues and envelope to the board until the project is complete. Blue Feather Products has a nifty product called the Piece Keeper. It is a metal bar that attaches to the wall or a cabinet. Pattern and fabric pieces are attached to the bar with colorful magnets. (See resource section.)

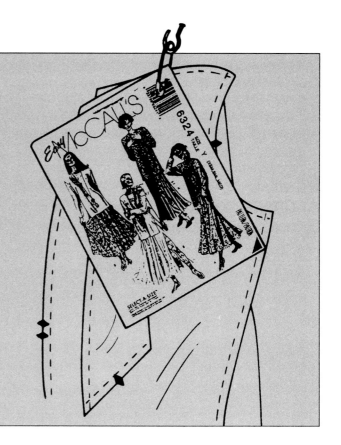

THREAD

Many of us come by our thread supply honestly—it was inherited. Our innate desire to collect thread in every color is a gene passed down from one generation to another! In all seriousness, most of us do have a thread collection and with the addition of the serger, that collection has not only grown, but has become more diverse in the size and style of the spool. In a sentence, thread has become more difficult to store. Let's look at ways to store thread.

Hanging and Countertop Racks

There are many wall-hanging racks available from your local sewing store or sewing mail-order catalogs. If wall space is at a premium, consider hanging the racks from the ceiling (see the resource section, page 122). Many interesting countertop models are also available.

Heritage Crafts

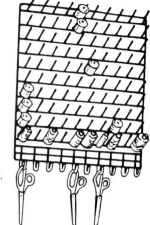

Dezzie Inc.

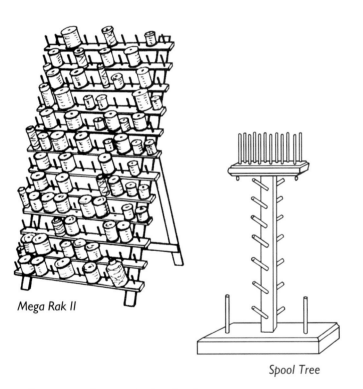

Mega Rak II

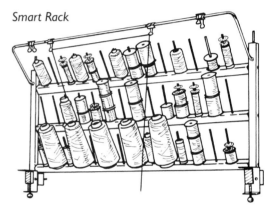

Smart Rack

Spool Tree

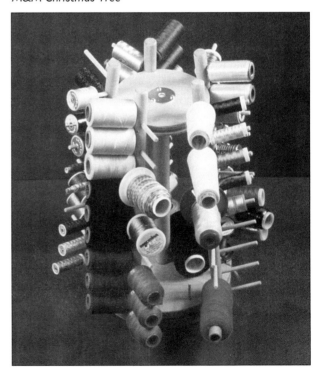

M&M Christmas Tree

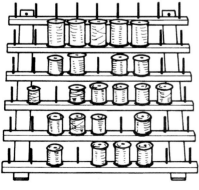

June Tailor
3-Way
Thread Rack

Cabinets & Drawers

Build a **custom wall storage** unit for thread. To keep dust-free, cover it with clear plastic or a fabric curtain.

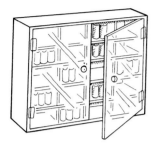

Note: Do not store thread where the sun beats in. Sun causes degradation of the fibers. Consider placing a unit like this in the space behind a door or even on the door, or perhaps on the back of a swinging closet door.

Drawers are great for storing thread. In closed drawers thread stays relatively dust-free and is protected from the elements. Use dividers to keep the thread organized in the drawer. A cutlery organizer tray would work. You can glue or tape heavy cardboard channels in the drawer to keep the thread tidy. Or use the step spice rack designed for kitchen cabinet drawers. It will hold the thread at a slight angle for ease of color matching.

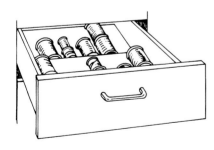

Or glue golf tees to a 1/8" piece of hardboard cut to fit in the drawer. Glued 2 3/4" apart, they become spool pins and hold the thread in place. Interior depth of the drawer should be at least 4".

Store thread in **specially designed drawer storage cabinets**. Carter's Workshop makes a beautiful thread chest (see resource section). You may want to have one designed and built for your collection.

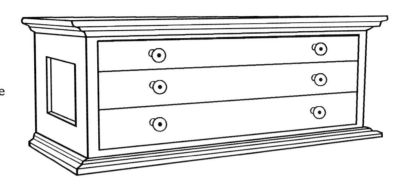

Pegboard

A painted pegboard organizing system can also be used for large put-up thread storage. Use the long extenders to hold three or four cones of thread. See pages 88 and 100 for examples of a variety of pegboards.

Antiques

♦ Antique spool chests are a fun and interesting way to store thread.

♦ Another ideal method of storing small put-ups of thread is in antique printer's drawers hung on the wall. These drawers are found in second-hand or antique stores. Screw them to the wall, level and plumb. They are aesthetically pleasing as well as practical—just hold the fabric up to the spools to find the best color of thread.

79

Boxes and Bags

Store thread in Ziploc bags, which in turn store in baskets or boxes. Consider decorating the boxes if they will be part of the decor on an open shelf. Sort thread according to type, such as cotton, silk, polyester, topstitching, quilting, embroidery, or according to put-up style, such as cones, king cones, tubes, or spools. You may need to take it one step further and sort the types into color families, too.

Note: If you like to keep thread spools and matching bobbins together, use a pipe cleaner, twisting the ends together.

Bobbin Storing

Many storage boxes are available for bobbins such as the Bob-N-Box, Bobbin Box, Bobbin Clip and magnetic bobbin holders that all keep the bobbins organized. Items that keep the bobbin attached to the spool of thread such as Handi-bobs and Bobbin Minders are also available.

Other ways to store bobbins include see-through plastic toothbrush holders used for traveling, ice-cube trays, medicine vials, embroidery floss organizers and desk-drawer organizers.

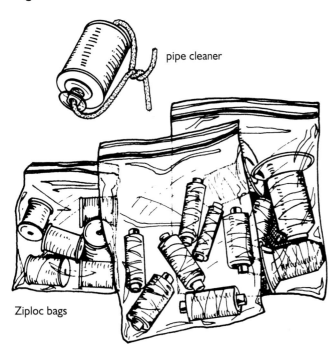

pipe cleaner

Ziploc bags

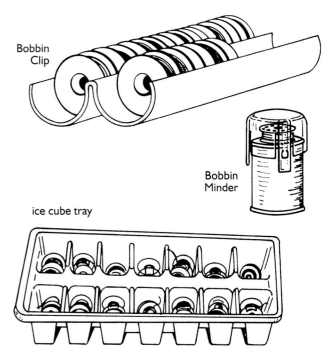

Bobbin Clip

Bobbin Minder

ice cube tray

Bob-N-Box

Plastic

Plastic storage containers can also be used for storing thread. Sort the thread according to size, use or fiber content. Label the boxes and store on shelves.

Plastic storage boxes with drawers can be used for thread storage as well as other small items. Hardware and discount stores carry them.

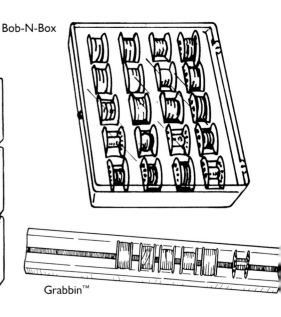

Grabbin™

BUTTONS AND OTHER SMALL NOTIONS

Button boxes bring back fond memories to many of us. I used to love to run my hands through my mother's button box and would spend hours sorting the buttons and enjoying the feel. However, the wonderful round tin container was not exactly an organizational prize. Also, fine antique or otherwise special buttons should not be allowed to rub against each other and there is potential for rust damage.

Let's look at ways to organize all our fabulous buttons.

♦ Make a button table. Use an antique printer's drawer (as mentioned for thread storage), mount it to a stool or table base (a piano bench base, for instance), fill the spaces with interesting buttons, cover with glass. When you want a button, simply remove the glass.

Note: You may want to run a strip of clear silicone caulking along the edge of the drawer to act as a buffer between the glass and the drawer. The silicone must cure before adding the glass, or the glass will be permanently sealed to the case! Marta used adhesive-backed Velcro® to attach the glass—little rounds on the corners of both glass and case.

♦ Antique and collectable buttons could be stored between layers of velvet. Make a book from pieces of velvet and stitch the buttons onto each page. Create an interesting work of art while you're at it! It can become **your** signature coffee table book!

♦ Buy an antique carpenter's toolbox or dental case. Both have many shallow drawers that will store unique buttons as well as any small tool such as X-Acto® knives, tweezers, button-hole cutters, scissors, etc.

Tins and canisters make attractive storage containers.

♦ There are many interesting clear containers that show off the buttons and organize them.

Lillian Vernon catalog item

Note: Buttons can be beautiful displayed in clear containers in a window, but make sure the window does not receive much direct sun, which will yellow the containers and the buttons!

♦ Apothecary and spice jars and their racks are an excellent button storage option. These free-standing or wall-mount systems work well for button, bead and sequin storage.

♦ Embroidery floss organizers work well for small buttons, snaps, sequins and beads. Similar boxes are sold in sporting goods stores as tackle boxes.

Embroidery floss organizers are also put to good use as sewing machine presser foot organizers. Make a reference chart and show each foot's name or number and the page number in the instruction book that explains the foot.

Note: Sewing mail-order companies offer a see-through plastic box with lift-out dividers to customize the compartments. This box is excellent for storage of sewing machine feet and accessories.

Mamma Ro storage box

- Rubbermaid has a fun snap-in system designed for the shop, but it works well in the sewing space. The system consists of various-sized containers with see-through tops and tool holders that hold scissors, screwdrivers, tweezers and other tools.

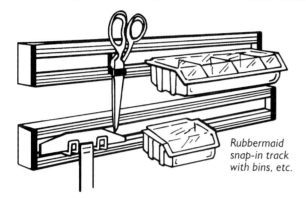

Rubbermaid snap-in track with bins, etc.

- Rubbermaid has many, many accessories that could be used to help organize small items in the sewing space. Many fit into drawers or can sit on small shelves. The key is to organize so you know what you have and can find it in a second.

- Store similar buttons in small Ziploc bags, which in turn are stored in a basket or bin. Further the organization by punching a hole at the top of the bags and slip like colors onto a single closing ring.

- Recycle plastic dividers from frozen dinners, cookies and other packaged foods for buttons, sequins, beads and other small items.

- Plastic breath-mint containers and clear 35 mm film canisters with snap-shut lids are perfect for small sequins, beads or snaps. The Bead and Bauble Stack Packs (available from mail order catalogs) are also a wonderful system.

- Fishing tackle boxes or tool boxes are great for storing small notions and tools. The bins can hold the tapes, rulers, glue, and scissors while the drawers hold safety pins, bodkins, thimbles, seam rippers, seam guides, bobbins, chalk, etc.

- Eagle Affiliates has designed a pleasing storage system called the CraftStor that is perfect for the crafter. (See resource section, page 122.)

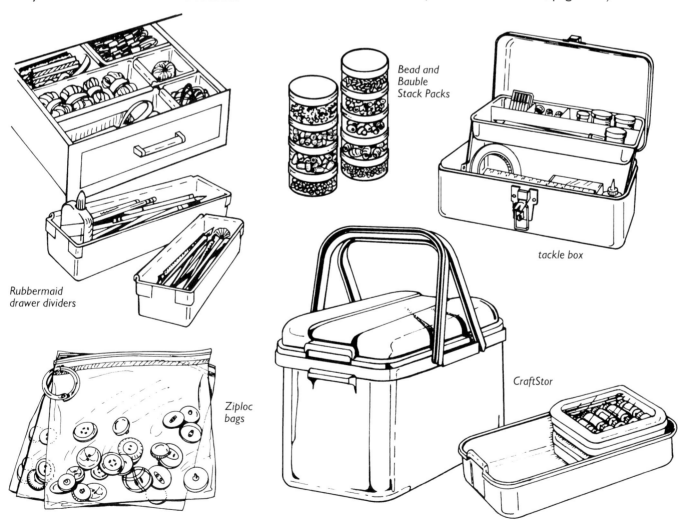

Rubbermaid drawer dividers

Bead and Bauble Stack Packs

tackle box

Ziploc bags

CraftStor

- Your local sewing store or sewing mail-order companies offer a unique organizer tray for tools and notions that pressure screws onto the edge of a table.

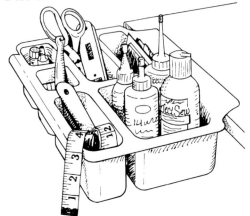

- June Tailor created a wall-hung organizer with many pockets, most of which are see-through vinyl. This organizer is perfect for your most-used notions, tools and patterns.

- Zippers can be hung on a swivel cup rack attached to a shelf or under a cabinet. Hang them by their zipper pulls according to size. Then all you need to do is spin the rack to find the zipper needed.

- Zippers can also be stored on a wire hanger. Using wire cutters, cut the hanger near where the wires join. Slip the zippers on.

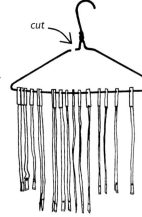

cut

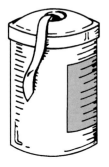

- Bulk elastic is easily stored in empty Baby Wipe containers. Enlarge the hole in the lid slightly and thread the elastic through it. No mess and no tangles.

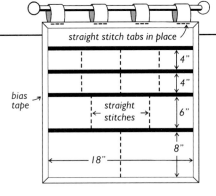

straight stitch tabs in place

bias tape

4"

4"

straight stitches

6"

8"

18"

Make Your Own Storage Caddy

Materials Needed
- 3/4 yd. sturdy fabric
- 3/4 yd. fusible web
- 3/4 yd. medium weight clear vinyl
- 20" long dowel rod
- 10 yds. bias tape

Cutting Directions

From Fabric:
- Cut 2 rectangles: 18"W x 26"L
- Cut 4 tabs for top: 4"W x 6"L

From Fusible Web:
- Cut 1 rectangle: 17 1/2"W x 25 1/2"L

From Vinyl:
- Cut 1 strip 18"W x 8"L
- Cut 1 strip 18"W x 6"L
- Cut 2 strips 18"W x 4"L

Sewing Procedure

1. Fuse web to wrong side of one 18" x 26" fabric rectangle. Peel paper backing from web and fuse to wrong side of remaining rectangle of fabric.

2. Finish the top and bottom edges of each vinyl strip using bias tape or a decorative 3-thread serger stitch. (Do not finish the bottom edge of the **bottom** piece of vinyl—finish only the top edge.)

Finish long edges.

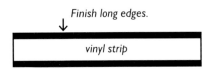

vinyl strip

3. Place vinyl strips as shown above. Stitch bottom of each strip to hold in place. (Do not pin into the vinyl! If slippage is a problem, use Scotch Magic Transparent Tape and do not leave it on for an extended amount of time.)

4. Finish the outer edges of the caddy using bias tape or a decorative serger stitch. Stitch around all four sides of the caddy, through all thicknesses, being sure to catch the side edges of the vinyl.

5. Straight stitch vertically through all thicknesses to create pockets.

6. Press the fabric tabs in half widthwise, wrong sides together, creating a tab 2"W x 6"L. Finish all four edges of each tab with bias tape or decorative serger stitch.

7. Fold tabs in half lengthwise and evenly space them along the wrong side of the top edge. Stitch in place.

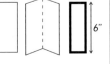

4"

2"

6"

From Winter '94 *Singer Sewing Basket* (Vol. III, #4)

PRESSING EQUIPMENT

All equipment relating to pressing should be stored by the press center.

- ♦ Consider a large basket under the pressing center on a shelf or on the floor.

- ♦ Plan a couple of drawers in the press center. (Be sure they are deep enough to store the ham!)

- ♦ Incorporate vertical storage in the press center for storage of large, flat items such as rotary-cutter mats.

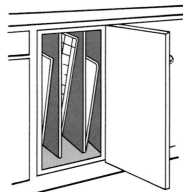

- ♦ Vegetable and fruit storage bins designed for the kitchen are an excellent addition to the press center for equipment storage.

SCISSORS, SHEARS AND OTHER CUTTING TOOLS

As with fine kitchen cutlery, the blades of your shears, scissors and rotary cutters should not be allowed to knock against each other. Also, scissors and shears should be stored closed to protect the cutting edges.

- ♦ The magnetic rack designed to hold fine kitchen cutlery is an excellent addition to the sewing space. The powerful magnet safely holds the blades of scissors, shears and even rotary cutters. It can be mounted on the wall either horizontally or vertically.

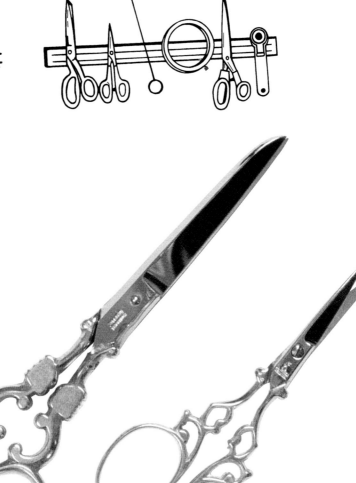

♦ The mug rack still has a place in the sewing space. It is an excellent way to store scissors and shears as well as other sewing supplies. If an item won't fit over the pegs, tie a ribbon to it.

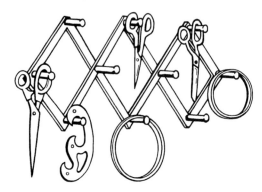

♦ Cutting tools can be stored in a drawer. Consider lining the drawer with flannel or felt to help protect the blades and to cut down on the movement of the items when the drawer is opened and shut. Or, protect the shears by slipping the closed blades into an eye glass case.

♦ A scissor block is available that resembles the knife block in your kitchen.

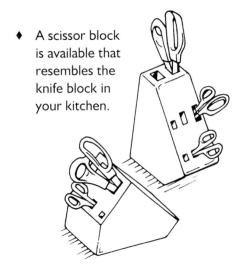

ON-THE-GO ORGANIZERS

♦ Sewing mail-order catalogs offer fun bags for sewing on-the-go. One style is designed to hold large and small notions, scissors, and patterns. Additional inserts are available too.

♦ Creative Carriers offers an entire line of wonderful carriers specially designed for anyone from crafter to quilter. (See resource section, pg. 122.)

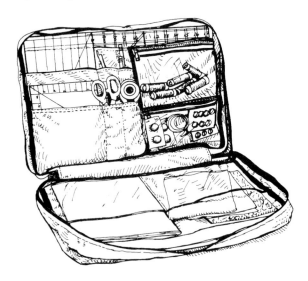

♦ Make your own carrier—Frost Line Kits has a pattern! (See resource section.)

♦ ♦ ♦

Attractive storage can make the difference between a pleasant sewing area and an overwhelming one.

A bookshelf in the shared guestroom/sewing space (see next page) is used to store sewing equipment with family mementos. An old fishing creel stores large spools of thread and a hand-turned burl-wood pot is filled with assorted sewing needles and notions.

A dining room bay window/sewing space (page 13) is a great place to use antiques for storage. The spool cabinet houses an assortment of threads and notions. The basket holds favorite fabrics, enriching the decor of the room before being turned into finished projects. The buffet is filled with fabric, sewing projects bagged and ready to start, pressing equipment...and the family silver. On top, Gail Brown's antique pincushions mingle with craft-store paper boxes used to store trims, notions and sewing "stuff."

Paula Marineau, who creates wearable art in Portland, Oregon, uses a window seat in her studio as a display area for a combination of interesting storage and artwork.

87

This guest room easily converts to a sewing room by folding up the Murphy bed and opening the sewing cabinets.

The sewing posters are by Linda McGehee. The collage art above the stack of suitcases is by Kelley Salber (see resource section). The hand-turned burl-wood bowl was made by my husband Paul.

ALL KINDS OF SEWING ALL AROUND THE HOUSE

Most of us do not have an area that we can claim exclusively for a sewing space. If we are lucky, we can use an extra bedroom, which sometimes must double as guest room or office. Often we share the room with other family activities. When all other space is claimed, we sometimes even turn to closets. Let's look at a number of small sewing spaces.

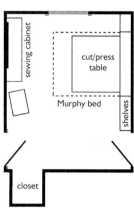

THE GUESTROOM AS SEWING ROOM

Even with a SMALL guest room, you can create an efficient sewing space. In the room shown here, the guest bed is a Murphy bed built into the wall, allowing enough floor space to sew. A cut/press table was designed to attach to the bottom of the Murphy bed. It folds up and locks into place so the bed can be lowered for guest use. Along the wall opposite the bed is a Roberts sewing cabinet that houses the sewing machine and serger. This sewing cabinet closes up easily, hiding the machines, and looks like a beautiful piece of furniture. A pile of old suitcases stores fabric and adds ambiance to the room. A section of pegboard artfully holds baskets and jars of sewing notions.

The Murphy Bed

A waterbed used to be set up in this guest room. The white bookcase-style cabinets had been installed to frame the waterbed. To make room for sewing, the waterbed was replaced with a Murphy bed. You can purchase a pre-made Murphy bed unit to install yourself or have installed for you, or you can make your own like we did here (see Appendix B, page 121 for the how-tos). The mattress for this Murphy bed is 4"-thick, medium-density foam. Foam was chosen for two reasons: the Murphy bed is not a standard bed size (it is between a twin and a double) and foam is lighter than a standard mattress, making it easier to raise and lower without fancy hardware.

Sewing in the Bedroom

If you cannot build a Murphy bed or otherwise get rid of the bed, then use it! In Gail Brown's sewing studio she simply places a rotary-cutting mat directly on the bed and uses the space under the bed for storage.

If you prefer a higher cutting surface, build a raised platform to place on the bed. Design the platform so the legs fold up and the entire unit can then be stored under the bed.

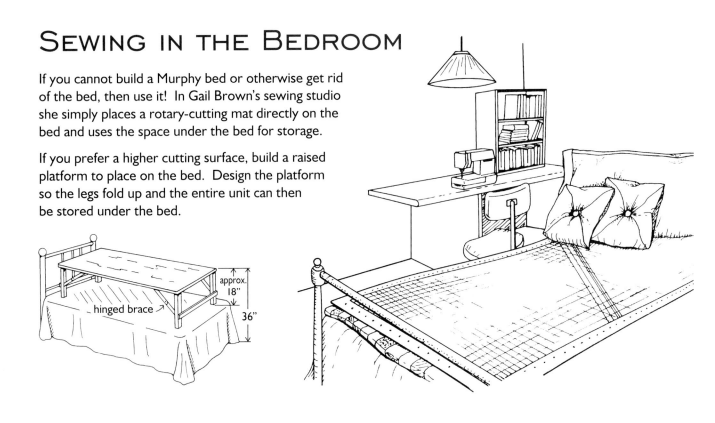

The Bedroom Converted

If you have a spare bedroom, make it into a sewing room, as Pati Palmer did with this room in her former home.

This extra bedroom lent itself well to a sewing space. The built-in shelves allowed for interesting decorating with the wall space above seemingly planned for two printer's drawers for thread storage! Note the bulletin board made of foam core covered with fabric, and the mug rack conveniently located next to the main sewing area. The table becomes the cutting area.

ANOTHER BEDROOM CONVERTED

Heirloom sewing is Debra Justice's love. Debra is an international speaker, teacher, designer, writer and founder of **Labours of Love Heirloom Sewing Supplies**, a Canadian mail-order company based in Abbotsford, B.C. Debra converted a spare bedroom into a sewing space with the use of cabinets and a countertop purchased from a home/building supply store. She applied her design talents to decorate the room, using paint, wallpaper and fabric, creating a sewing space that reveals and revels in heirloom's beauty.

The sewing center is simply a length of countertop supported on each end by tall units, one of which is used for hanging space and the other for storage. Under-cabinet lights illuminate the center, and storage is created above with wall-hung cabinets. Debra uses a Sew/Fit folding cardboard table for her cutting center, seen in the top left photo.

THE LAUNDRY ROOM

Joanne Di Benedetto-Burdick looked to her laundry room when she wanted to create sewing space. Her well-insulated and heated basement houses the family laundry and storage rooms, so it was a natural for her to carve out space for her sewing. Joanne designed her space so she is still a part of the family's activities in the adjoining family room, while efficiently using her what-little-spare-time-she-has to sew.

Joanne is a kitchen and bath designer who reps a cabinet line, so she created her space using the cabinets she represents. She designed in two deep file drawers for pattern storage, roll-out shelves for fabric storage, an ironing board in a drawer, and a deep drawer for pressing equipment below it. She also installed the cabinets 6" away from the wall for extra-deep counter surfaces. Since she wants to take her sewing cabinets with her to her newly designed (by

her architect father) home, she chose not to install the cabinets to the wall nor to install the cabinet's toe kicks. Without the toe kicks this bonus space can be used to store bolts of interfacing and fabric (wrapped in plastic).

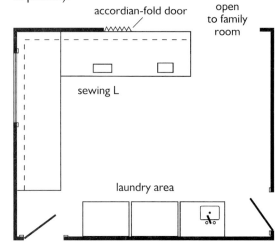

OFFICE/SEWING SPACE

Linda Wisner, design director for Palmer/Pletsch and co-author of *Creative Serging for the Home and Other Quick Decorating Ideas*, uses one of the bedrooms in her 1906 home as a combined sewing/graphics studio and office. Her design/sewing projects are very eclectic, ranging from fashion garments and wearable art to home decorating, craft projects and a line of stuffed-animal patterns. As a designer, her design tools are as important as her sewing tools. The room combines them all, colorfully, and accessibly. Out of sight to the right are computer, fax machine, file cabinets, light table and desk...all in a room only 12'x14'.

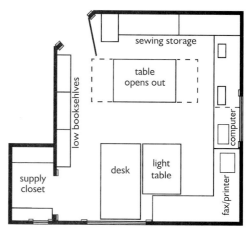

From Dining Room to Sewing Room & Office

My sewing space/office is quite small. It would be a great size if it were dedicated only to sewing, but the room must also serve as my home office. Originally the dining room, the space was converted to a much-needed sewing/office area during a kitchen remodel that created an eating area.

In analyzing my time and needs, I concluded that most of my sewing time is spent doing home-decorating projects, sewing children's clothing and creating gifts and crafts. When I took stock of my sewing belongings, I discovered I had about anything and everything ever made for sewing, and have been or am involved in every popular craft project. I need storage for it all!

My biggest challenge, however, was dealing with home-decorating items. Home decorating requires the use of yards and yards of fabric. A small space offers a challenge for dealing with all that fabric, not to mention the notions, tools and hardware. As co-author of Palmer/Pletsch's book *Creative Serging for the Home and Other Quick Decorating Ideas*, I had collected every interesting swag holder, notion, and window treatment gadget I found. Storage of these items also became a challenge.

The living areas of my home are all open to each other, which I prefer because I can keep an eye on my two young daughters and feel a part of the family while sewing. However, there is a down side to this arrangement. Since the room is open to other living areas, I feel the need to keep the room neat and tidy, and the noise level can really escalate at times!

Before we get into how I store my collections, let's discuss the room layout. The room has many long windows, dictating the use of a one-wall layout. I did shorten one window to expand the work surface. Since the windows are double-hung, shortening is inexpensive and simple to do—just cut down the bottom frame and have new glass made for it. This small alteration allowed the use of modular 18" and 27" drawer bases, and 48" of open kneehole space for my sewing machine and serger. On the opposite wall from the sewing center is the computer center, which will be discussed later.

The office wall is opposite the sewing wall. My husband created a shelf over my computer and monitor to hold the telephone/fax and a battery back-up unit for the computer. (When you live in the country, electricity can be erratic.) The printer sits next to the monitor. The keyboard lives in the desk drawer under the monitor. To use it I simply raise it up on two check-book boxes...it works great!

well in the space between the window seat and the door to the food pantry. When I am working on a small project I use the table in it's smallest state. However, for children's clothing and larger projects, one section is flipped up creating a surface of 40"x45". For home-decorating projects, the table is wheeled out of the corner, into the common area between the sewing space and the kitchen and used in its full length of 72".

For sewing large pieces of home decorating fabric to create a project, I pull out the top drawer to the left of the sewing machine and place a 1/8"-thick piece of hardboard on the drawer edges. This creates an additional counter surface for which to rest fabric.

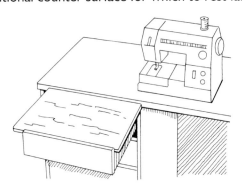

Note the high shelf above the windows. This shelf provides an additional 14 linear feet of storage. I store cotton scraps, felt and other small cuts of fabric for quilting and craft projects, ribbons and bias tape, zippers, and elastic in plastic bins and baskets. Beautiful Coats & Clark tins are used for snaps, Velcro, buttons and other closures.

Mounted below the shelf and in front of each window is a wooden closet rod. These rods serve as hanging space for projects in the works. They are especially nice for hanging sections of home decorating projects. (A slide screen is mounted in the far left window, which aids in planning seminars that feature a slide presentation.)

A large cutting area is essential for creating home-decorating projects. The room is much too small to have a permanent large surface, so I chose to use a fold-down cut/press table. In its smallest state it measures 40" wide by 19" deep and is 36" high and fits

A spice rack drawer insert works beautifully to store thread.

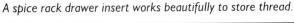

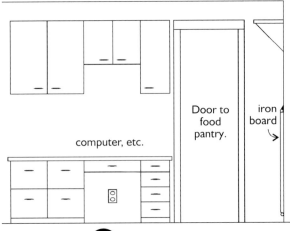

A OFFICE WALL

If the serger is needed for large, bulky projects, I either switch the serger and sewing machine or unplug the sewing machine and place it below the countertop.

I like my machines placed on top of the countertop rather then set on a lowered platform, because it allows the space to be more versatile. There are times when I need a large unbroken counter for layout and design—I simply unplug the machines and place them below the counter.

When creating small craft projects that require sewing and pressing, I set up the ironing board at 28" high and place it to the left of the machine. Then I can simply swing around in the chair to press, then swing back to sew.

To house my collection of home-decorating notions, fabric and samples, I borrowed a couple of shelves in the food pantry. I also borrow space under my bed for storage of needlework canvas, thread and ideas, as well as holiday craft projects. To keep track of my fabric stash, I keep a notebook in which I staple a square of fabric to a page, with the width, yardage, care instructions, fiber content listed and where the fabric is stored (e.g. under the bed, on the pantry shelf, in an empty suitcase...).

In times when more counter space is needed, I use my ironing board. In fact, I use it as a buffet during large get-togethers. I cover it with a tablecloth and have an extra counter!

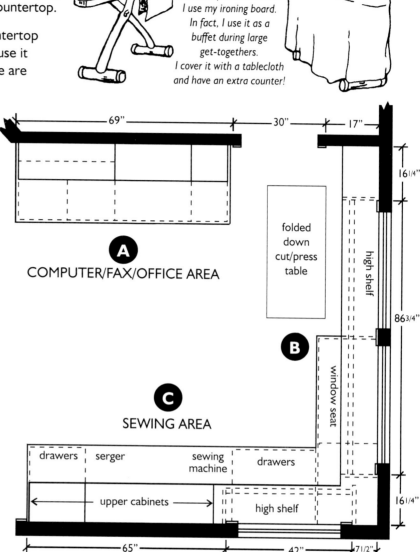

A COMPUTER/FAX/OFFICE AREA

folded down cut/press table

high shelf

B

window seat

C SEWING AREA

drawers | serger | sewing machine | drawers

upper cabinets

high shelf

69" 30" 17" 16 1/4" 86 3/4" 16 1/4"

65" 42" 7 1/2"

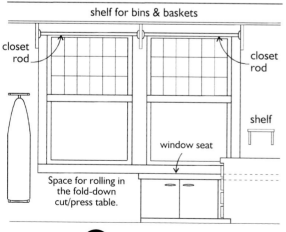

shelf for bins & baskets

closet rod

closet rod

shelf

window seat

Space for rolling in the fold-down cut/press table.

B WINDOW WALL

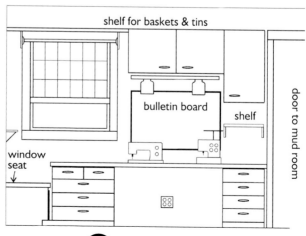

shelf for baskets & tins

bulletin board

shelf

window seat

door to mud room

C SEWING WALL

97

BUILD YOUR OWN SPACE

As mentioned earlier, some sewing-cabinet companies manufacture an array of cabinets that can be combined to form a small yet functional sewing space. These cabinets can be closed up to give the appearance of furniture such as an entertainment center. However, in the interest of money or customization, you may choose to make your own.

The design shown on this page is modeled after a unit originally designed by Marta Alto's father. Marta used her father's creation for many years. Build as six separate units and screw together to install.

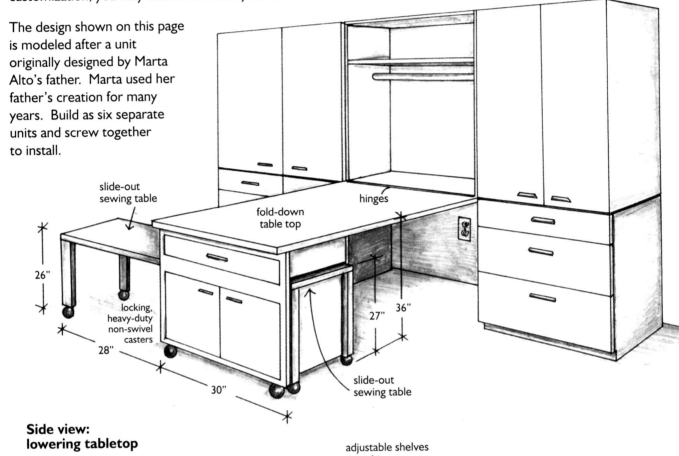

slide-out sewing table

fold-down table top

hinges

26"

locking, heavy-duty non-swivel casters

28"

30"

27"

36"

slide-out sewing table

Side view: lowering tabletop

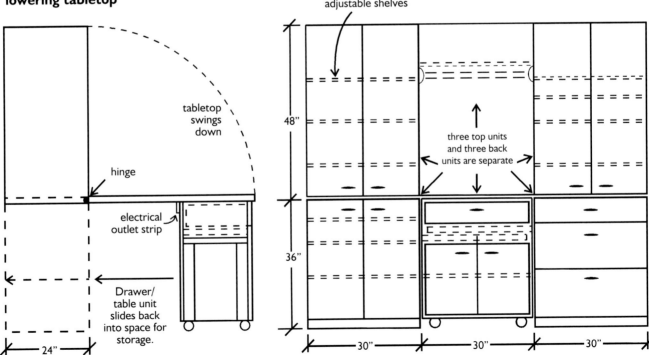

adjustable shelves

tabletop swings down

hinge

electrical outlet strip

Drawer/ table unit slides back into space for storage.

24"

48"

three top units and three back units are separate

36"

30"

30"

30"

Naomi Baker's son built her the sewing unit below as his first woodworking experience! Naomi is a popular sewing instructor and an author of several books on sergers and projects created with the serger. Her sewing space is located in the family room of her home in Springfield, Oregon, which also functions as the office/computer space. A true family room! (See page 111 for information on computer setup.)

Naomi uses a Create-a-Space table for cutting; book shelves in the hall for book, video and magazine storage; and a large wicker chest for storage of projects and samples, which are individually packaged in Ziploc bags. The wicker chest also serves as a coffee table.

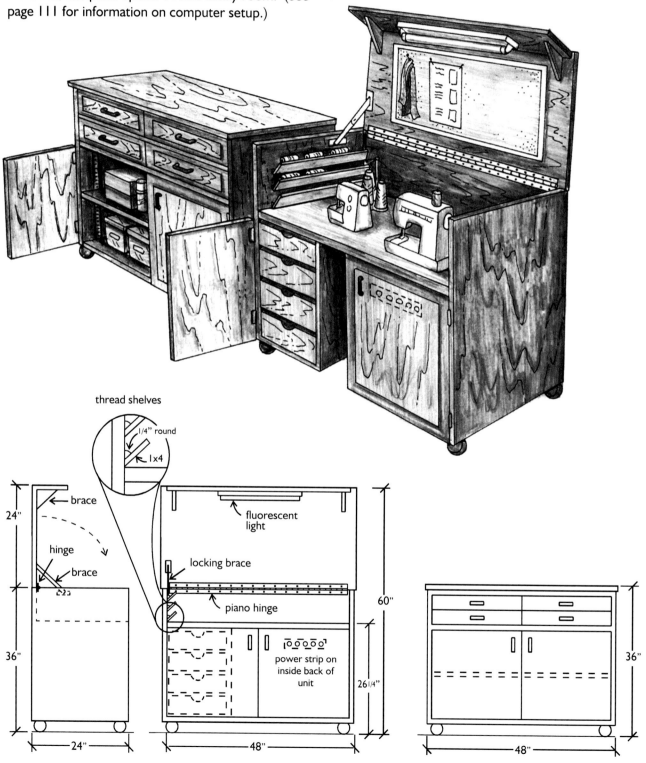

thread shelves

1/4" round

1x4

brace

24"

hinge

brace

36"

fluorescent light

locking brace

piano hinge

60"

power strip on inside back of unit

26 1/4"

24"

48"

36"

48"

WHEN ALL YOU HAVE IS A CLOSET

Perhaps all you can claim is a closet for your sewing space. Closets can function beautifully as small, yet efficient sewing areas. Since sliding doors prohibit efficient use of the space, take them off. Treat the opening like a window and create or purchase a window treatment to close it off or consider switching to swinging doors or bifolds.

A Closet with Fold-Out Table

This small bedroom closet was converted into an efficient sewing area. Adjustable shelves hold Rubbermaid bins labeled as to their contents. A painted plywood countertop installed in the closet serves as the serger sewing center. Large project baskets store under the countertop. Pegboard lines the walls between the countertop and shelves to store scissors, notions and thread (the spools were threaded onto craft wire which is hung on a peg). A fold-down table was mounted to the back of the closet door, and serves as the main sewing area, but can also be used for cutting and layout. A dowel system was built and attached to the door to store lengths of fabric.

The swing-down table seen in the photographs is mounted to the door higher than the inside countertop, allowing door to swing closed over the countertop. When the table is swung up, a ledge just wide enough for the machine allows it to remain there for storage. A swivel-neck task light is mounted to the shelf, too, so it never has to be moved!

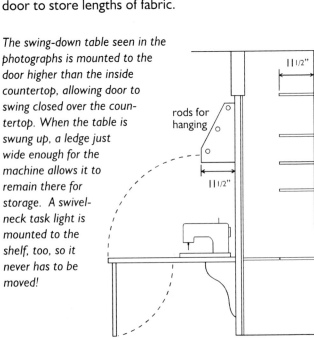

The closet featured on the previous page has a swinging door on which a table is mounted. Here are three closets with bi-fold doors:

This may well be the most cost-effective way to convert a closet into a simple sewing space. A countertop was installed the entire width of the closet, allowing the space underneath to be used for storage. Shelves were installed on the wall, pegboard lines the side wall, a thread rack, narrow shelves and bulletin board share the back wall. Install good lights in the closet—the best would be an adjustable one on each side wall.

This closet works nicely when only one machine is used. More storage is possible when using this design. Ready-to-assemble storage units available in building supply stores are combined here to provide drawers of varying sizes for storage. Office supply and housewares stores were the source of the other containers used to store sewing supplies and a cache of old sewing magazines—a wonderful inspiration source!

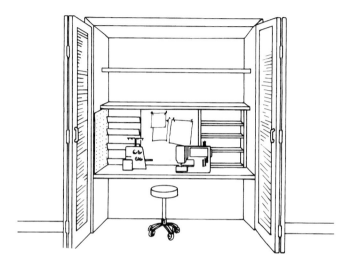

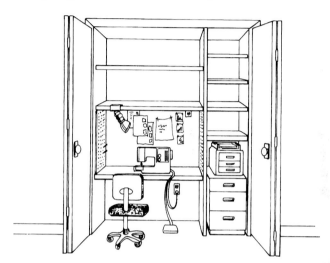

Nancy Zieman designed this small closet sewing space. It, too, features a fold-down table, but this time the table folds down from inside the closet, rather than from the door. When not in use, the machines are placed on a shelf in the closet. If you choose this style, try to plan your space so your most often-used items (the ones you seem to need every day, such as scissors and pins) are easy to reach by opening only one door (not behind the table).

The closet featured on page 100 is a single swinging door. If you have a double door closet, you could hang an ironing board from a caddy mounted to the door. Above it, mount a "pocket" of wood to hold pressing ham, sleeve roll and press cloths. A chest of drawers adds extra storage and the mirror mounted above it creates a small fit area. Mount a closet rod between the shelves and the side wall to create a hanging space.

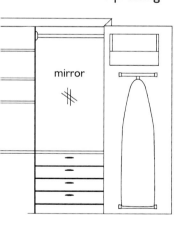

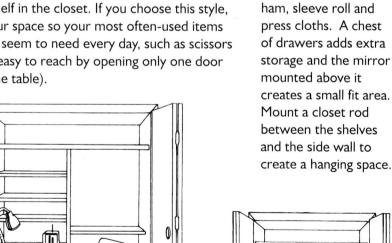

table down   table up

Using Every Nook & Cranny

Efficient use of small space is vital when you are trying to carve out a sewing area in a home that is already filled with the other pieces of your life. Nooks and crannies can be found everywhere. Here are a few ideas on what to do with them.

♦ Don't forget the space above the doors and windows for extra storage. Install a 10-12"-deep shelf above the molding of windows and doors. If the room is small and enclosed, paint the shelf the same or a slightly lighter color as the walls. This keeps the room from visually caving in. Store not-as-often-used items in bins, wooden boxes, baskets and/or tins and place them on the shelf. Books can also be stored up there; just make sure the shelf is supported well and secure.

♦ Don't forget the backs of doors and/or the wall space behind doors.
Be sure to use a door stop to prevent damage to the wall or goodies stored there should an overzealous person swing open the door.

Many behind-the-door storage units are available from variety stores, including towel racks mounted to the door's hinges and over-the-door garment hooks.

Mount cork board to the back of the door to serve as a bulletin board.

If wall space is at a premium, mount your full-length mirror on the back of your sewing room door.

Mount thread racks to the wall behind the door.

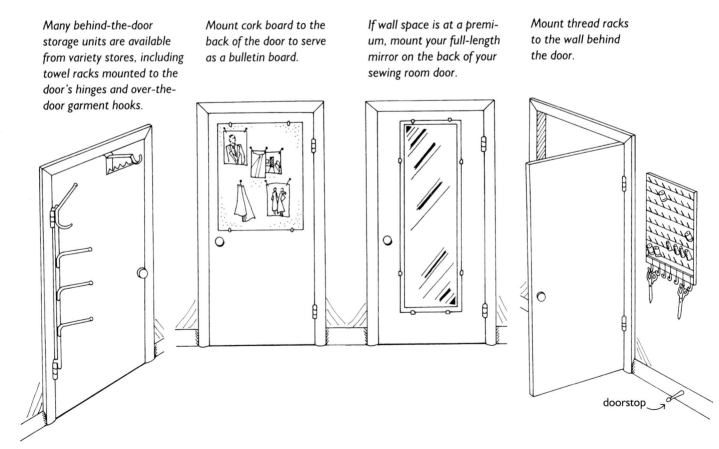

doorstop

◆ Plan a pullout landing space (like a bread board) in cabinets. This can serve as an extra counter and can even create an efficient "U" layout if planned on each side of the sewing machine. This pullout can also be valuable in the cut/press center as an extra counter for staging, scissors, pins, etc.

◆ When baskets and wire bins are used for storage in tall cabinets, a pullout landing space is very handy when you need to sort through a bin.

◆ Look at unusual spaces and analyze if they are being used efficiently. For instance, what is under the staircase? Is the space being efficiently used with shelves, hooks, and other storage helps? Could the "stuff" be stored more efficiently somewhere else, freeing up the space for a sewing area?

◆ Strategically placed mirrors can make a room seem larger!

◆ Use the space "lost" between studs. Cut out the wallboard and install shelves to store thread, magazines, etc. If your home is 2x4 construction, the shelf depth will be about 3"—just enough for storing serger thread on tubes or cones. You could also install wooden dowels for hanging fabric or wooden strips for creating magazine racks. Do not use this idea on exterior walls, though, because they have insulation in them. And know where your electrical wires and plumbing pipes are—do not cut into the wall unless you know nothing is there!

## CHAPTER 9

SPECIALTY SEWING

Different types of sewing require a different usage of space. For instance, the home decorator and bridal sewer need large cutting surfaces. These two types of professionals, as well as the dressmaker, may also have to consider space for one or more industrial machines, clients coming into their home, and more than one person using the sewing studio. The storage requirements may also be different. Let's look at the specialty sewer's requirements.

Multiple People Using the Sewing Space

If more than one person is using the sewing space, allow an unobstructed working path or triangle for each person. If your business doesn't require each person to have access to each work area, adjust your plan accordingly. Perhaps one person just does the layout and design, needing access to the layout board or wall, computer, and desk. Another person does the cutting, needing to use fabric storage and cutting supplies, and the third person does the sewing, requiring the use of machines, thread and sewing supplies. Separate work triangles are not needed. However, if the jobs overlap with more than one person sewing and pressing, each person needs a work triangle to him- or herself.

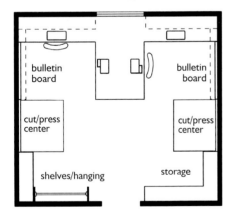

Large Cutting Surface

A large cutting surface is a necessity for many professionals. You may have a sewing space large enough to incorporate the table, or you may need to designate a different room just for cutting. If so, be sure to have doubles of needed notions so you don't spend unnecessary energy running back and forth between rooms.

Machine Requirements

The more machines, the more space is required. There is no way around this. For an inexpensive, multiple home-machine layout, just use countertop material and cleat to the wall. Then add support panels and simply line up the machines on the counter. Try to arrange an L or U format for efficiency. Use a double-thickness countertop (two pieces of 3/4" pressboard covered with laminate rather than just one). When spanning large amounts of space, the double thickness will be more stable and you'll get less machine vibration.

Storage Requirements

If your business requires a lot of storage, consider using industrial metal shelves to create bays—like a library. These shelves can store boxes and bins of notions, bolts of fabric, machines, books, etc. Place the shelves singly or back to back. Create as many bays as you need. If desired, drape the space off from the rest of the room with curtains mounted to rods or metal tracks (like a hospital bed drape).

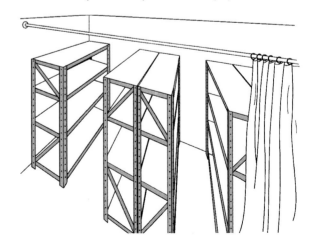

PROFESSIONAL DRESSMAKER

client waiting area

Part of the dressmaker's talents lie in helping create a special, personal look for each of her clients, so the decor and feel of the studio is of utmost importance. The studio must enhance that dream as well as enhance your professionalism.

Keep in mind what the client sees when she enters the studio. When designing the space, plan lots of hidden storage with just a few open areas for creating aesthetically pleasing displays.

Try to plan a reception area. It doesn't have to be much; just a comfortable, welcoming area—perhaps an antique treadle sewing machine with a colorful basket of thread and a chair in an area just inside the studio entrance, with current fashion magazines in a near-by magazine rack.

The professional also needs a private or semi-private fitting area complete with a three-way mirror.

Multiple machines are a reality and space must be given for most of them. Rarely used, special machines may be stored under the counter and easily brought up for use.

Finally, as large a cutting area as possible must be planned in the design, as well as ways to stay organized when creating many garments for many clients.

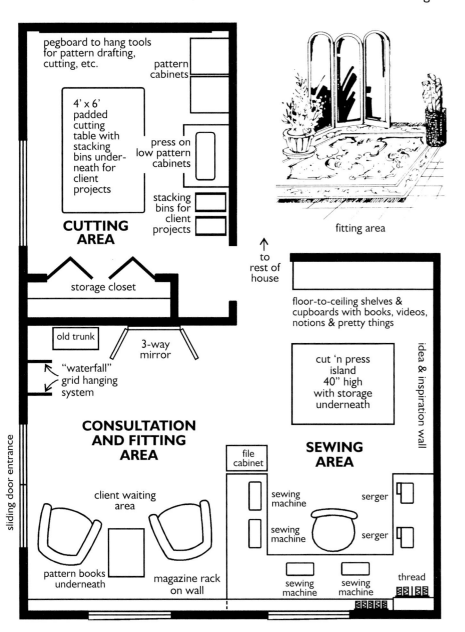

pegboard to hang tools for pattern drafting, cutting, etc.

pattern cabinets

4' x 6' padded cutting table with stacking bins underneath for client projects

press on low pattern cabinets

stacking bins for client projects

CUTTING AREA

storage closet

old trunk

3-way mirror

"waterfall" grid hanging system

CONSULTATION AND FITTING AREA

client waiting area

pattern books underneath

magazine rack on wall

sliding door entrance

fitting area

↑ to rest of house

floor-to-ceiling shelves & cupboards with books, videos, notions & pretty things

cut 'n press island 40" high with storage underneath

idea & inspiration wall

file cabinet

SEWING AREA

sewing machine

sewing machine

sewing machine

sewing machine

serger

serger

thread

*This studio layout was designed for Kathleen Spike, professional dressmaker and the first national chairman of the Professional Association of Custom Clothiers. Kathleen is an internationally renowned speaker, author of **Sew to Success**, **How to Make Money in a Home-Based Sewing Business**, and star of its accompanying video **Sewing to Success**, in which you can view her studio live. The space was originally a "mother-in-law apartment." Kathleen's cutting area is in a separate room, away from view. A reception area is just inside the door. To the left of the door is a grid rack to store finished garments. An illustration of it can be found on page 66.*

BRIDAL SEWING

The bridal sewer is a specialized professional dressmaker, who has even more specific needs. The bridal dressmaker is not just sewing wedding gowns and bridesmaid dresses, she is creating a dream. The studio is a big part of setting the stage. It is extremely important that the studio be clean, tidy and pleasingly decorated. Picture this...the bride-to-be enters the room and is met with the gown hanging from a chain from the ceiling (use a bosom hanger for a more realistic look). If there is a train, it is spread out. What bride wouldn't love the work you just did?

A bridal fitting area should be at least 4' x 6'. It should include a large-as-possible three-way mirror and good lighting. Also needed in that area is comfortable seating for the mother or friend who accompanies the bride-to-be to the fittings. Consider raising the fitting area 9" from the floor.

Plan a noncrushing hanging space for nearly-finished garments waiting for final fittings and as temporary storage of the completed gowns. In the floorplan below, three hooks mounted on the wall above the window swing down when needed.

Many bridal gowns and bridesmaid dresses are full length, so working on the hems or beading, ruffles, lace and other embellishments at the bottom of the dress can be a big pain in the back. Therefore, you must consider a way to raise the dress so it is more easily worked on. A simple answer is to hang a chain from a hook in the ceiling. The hanger can be hung from any link in the chain, raising the dress to a more comfortable level.

In the floorplan below, the closet is designed to be the fitting area with mirrors swinging out from the door frame and a large mirror installed on the back wall. The side mirrors can be positioned for best viewing by the client. When a fitting is not in process, roll in tall wire racks equipped with baskets for storage of fabric scraps, findings, interfacing, etc.

The floorplan here and on the next page are basically the same room, each modified slightly to meet the special needs of the bridal and home dec seamstress. Both need room to handle lots of yards of fabric, plus space to hang large finished projects.

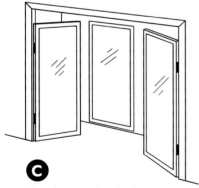

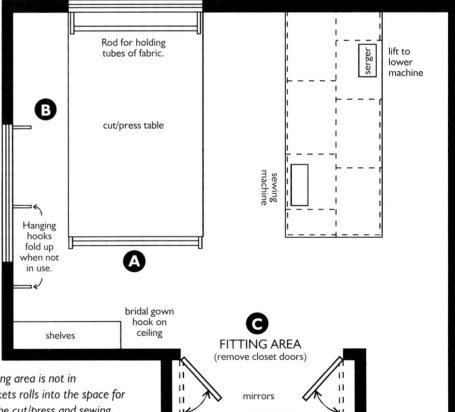

C

The closet is also the fitting area. One mirror is centered on the back wall of the closet. The other two are hinged to the door frame. When the fitting area is not in use, a tall rolling rack equipped with baskets rolls into the space for storage. Roll it into the space between the cut/press and sewing centers during fitting sessions.

Home Decorating

The needs of the home-dec seamstress vary a bit from the professional dressmaker in that many yards of fabric are needed for interior work. Interior seamstresses think in terms of bolts instead of yards! A large cutting space with special accessories is needed to make this process (which is the most important step of home decorating) as comfortable as possible, leaving the mind clear for concise thinking.

Since the decorator usually goes to the client's home to take the necessary measurements before starting a project and to install the finished goods at the end, the decor of the studio is not as important as it is for the professional dressmaker. What is important in the studio is a staging area for partially completed projects and those completed and waiting for delivery.

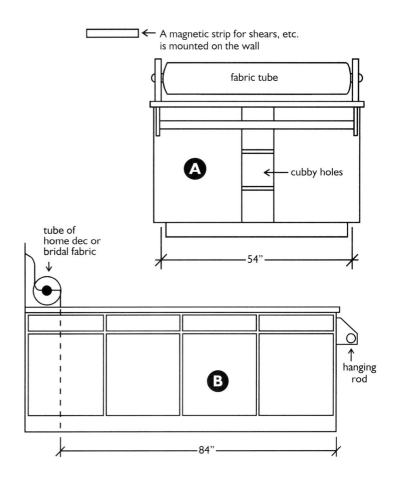

A magnetic strip for shears, etc. is mounted on the wall

fabric tube

A

cubby holes

tube of home dec or bridal fabric

54"

B

hanging rod

84"

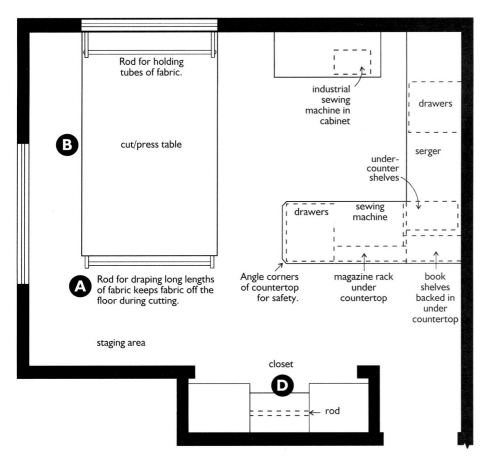

Rod for holding tubes of fabric.

B

cut/press table

industrial sewing machine in cabinet

drawers

serger

under-counter shelves

drawers

sewing machine

A Rod for draping long lengths of fabric keeps fabric off the floor during cutting.

Angle corners of countertop for safety.

magazine rack under countertop

book shelves backed in under countertop

staging area

closet

D

rod

This space is an extra bedroom in the house (as is the bridal floorplan). In this case a more efficient U layout is used for the sewing center. Either layout could be used.

The design of the closet creates compartments for large project bins to hold the fabric for each project, along with hardware, tools and other "stuff." In this room the closet is the primary storage area.

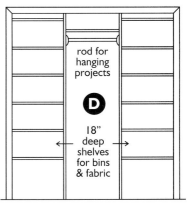

rod for hanging projects

D

18" deep shelves for bins & fabric

QUILTING

The quilter may do home decorating or fashion sewing. The quilter of home decorating has some of the same needs as that of the home decorator except the fabric yardage is less per piece, but many more pieces are used!

A planning and layout area is needed, perhaps even with a drawing table added. Hang rigid Styrofoam insulation covered with heavy quilt batting, felt or flannel on the wall to create a design and layout wall. Large expanses of countertop are needed around the machines to support the quilt as it is stitched together.

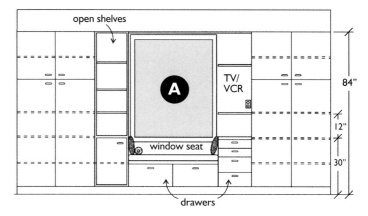

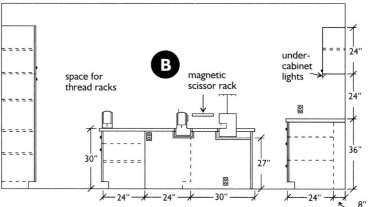

Note:
Remember, perspectives like the one to the right may help you visualize the space, but elevations and floorplans like the ones on this page are needed for the cabinet maker.

This room was designed for an avid quilter.

Section A *is a series of cabinets serving as a storage wall. A built-in window seat, complete with a TV/VCR unit, was designed with the husband or child in mind.*

Section B *is the sewing center. The main sewing area is the L-shape where the primary sewing machine and serger are located. The less often used machine is across the peninsula.*

Section C *is the pressing center. It's deep counter-top has a cut/press board on it and the narrow section is for the press.*

Section D *is the layout table and design wall.*

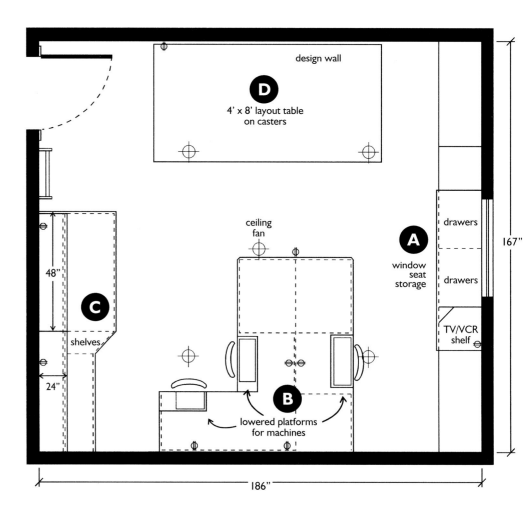

Storage for the Quilter

Jean Wells of Sisters, Oregon, suggests the use of new pizza boxes to store fabric precut into quilt blocks. Store according to color, and label the ends of the boxes. (See pages 71-73 and 110 for more fabric storage ideas.)

Scraps of batting can also be hard to store. Invest in attractive, large wicker hampers or old blanket chests. Under the bed works nicely too!

A large, well organized closet can create order out of the many bits and scraps of fabric a quilter uses. Shallow shelves are best, as it is easy to loose small items in dark recesses. The closet illustrated here offers optimum accessibility by having swing out shelf units attached to the door frame. (The doors to the closet have been removed.)

hinges

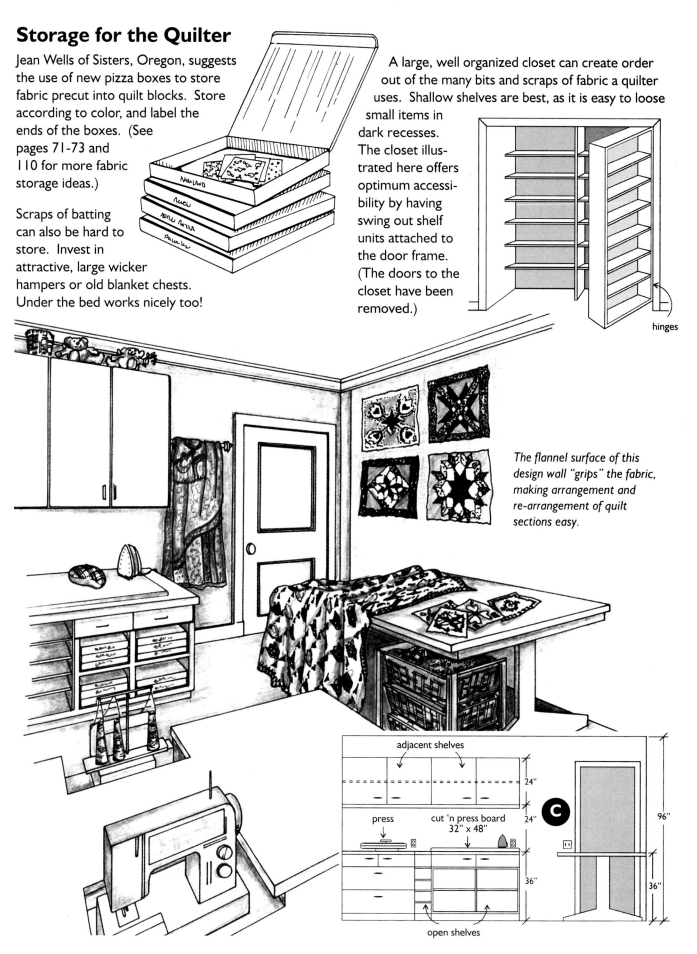

The flannel surface of this design wall "grips" the fabric, making arrangement and re-arrangement of quilt sections easy.

adjacent shelves

press

cut 'n press board 32" x 48"

24"

24"

36"

96"

36"

C

open shelves

CRAFTING & WEARABLE ART

The crafter and creator of wearable art both need lots of storage for many little things—numerous cuts of fabric, paints, markers, stamps, threads and ribbons, buttons, beads, sequins, and just about any interesting bauble that catches your eye! Organization is extremely important. You must know where everything is and store everything in a logical manner. Many storage ideas have already been discussed, but here are a few more:

♦ Use wood dowels, tie, wine, or mug racks to hang strips of fabric.

♦ Use divided cardboard or wood boxes, like the Pepsi box below, to store rolled pieces of fabric.

♦ To store large spools of thread, bottles of dye, glue bottles, etc., on deep shelves, place items on a tray that can be pulled out. The tray can even be taken to a workspace when needed.

♦ Use vinyl shoe organizers and fold or roll fabric into each pocket.

♦ Use drawers and divide with wire baskets or bins to keep items organized. This allows you to slip the entire bin or basket out of the drawer to be taken to the work area.

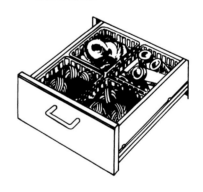

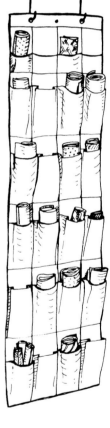

Designing in the Electronic Age

Computers and scanners are playing a larger part in design of craft, sewing and other textile projects. New software is being developed all the time. If you plan to add this kind of equipment to your sewing space keep in mind the guidelines on the next page as you design your space.

Computers

Many homes now have at least one computer and often this computer shares room space with the sewing machines. For some this is intentional because the computer interfaces with the sewing machine, but for many of us, it is a necessity of space sharing. The computer has certain requirements that must be met, especially if it is used for a home-based business.

Electrical

The computer, monitor and printer should be on their own circuit and protected with a surge protector. If the computer setup is part of an entire system of office equipment, allow another circuit for the fax machine, telephone answering machine, copier, etc. This means if your space is home to all of your sewing equipment as well as your home office-equipment, five circuits should be dedicated to that space! Consider adding a separate electrical panel to handle the needs.

Lighting

Lighting requirements for a computer are different from sewing. You **can** have too much light, which then reflects or glares off surfaces and causes squinting. Squinting leads to eye strain and headaches. Also, the shifting of your body, neck and head to avoid the glare can cause neck pain, back pain, muscle tension and fatigue.

A computer monitor emits light from the screen (like a flashlight), so a lower level of general light is needed in this part of the work space. The screen also has a reflective quality (like a mirror), so room lights must be placed to avoid their reflecting from the screen into the operator's eyes. Incandescent lighting is the best choice for the computer space and putting the light on a dimmer switch will help individualize needed light. Task lights can be used to help with the light needed for related tasks that occur near the computer. Just make sure to shine the light away from the screen. The light from windows can appear as reflections or glare in the screen. Locate the screen so its back is to the window—not so the window is to the side or front of the screen. When the sun is strong, lower the window treatment.

Chair

A chair just like the one described on page 30 is necessary, but this time you may want to tilt the seat pan back about five degrees from level to enable you to take advantage of the lumbar support in the backrest. If you feel pressure on the back of your legs, or if your feet do not comfortably reach the floor, add a foot rest. A good foot rest should not shift or move while being used, should have a nonskid surface, and should be wide enough for both feet. A foot rest is more comfortable if the surface is angled up to 15 degrees toward the toes.

Work Surface

Tasks at the computer terminal and keyboard are best accomplished if your forearms are held at a 75- to 90-degree angle to your upper arms. The eye-to-screen distance should allow you to easily see all of the characters on the screen without making you lean your head and body forward or backward. Locate the monitor at a height that allows you to hold your head in a normal posture and just move your eyes to see the characters. One commonly used rule is to position the screen so the center is about level with your chin.

Note: It is impossible to give an exact eye-to-screen distance because of the many variables involved: work-surface heights and depths, location of the work station in the room, monitor sizes and shapes, and variations in individuals themselves. A generous range would be 14-30".

forearms held at 75°-90° angle to upper arms

Computer needs to be placed to the left or right of a window.

TEACHING

Because of the lack of classroom space in fabric stores, many private sewing instructors teach classes in their own studio.

Obviously, the cost to create a classroom in a basement, garage, spare bedroom or family room is important to consider. Let's look at ideas on how to set up a classroom in your space.

Electrical needs can be one of the most difficult and expensive parts of a sewing school. An alternative to adding electrical outlets is to use power tracks. A power track is located above counter level around the outer perimeter of the room. It is a long track that supports movable outlets. The wire within the track is shielded, and well-hidden. This electrical system is ideal in classroom situations where equipment is frequently moved. Power tracks can be purchased from electrical supply houses. As mentioned in the electrical chapter, make sure your home's wiring can handle the added load of multiple machines and pressing centers. Check with a qualified electrical contractor to add circuits or power to your home. You may even consider adding an entirely separate electrical panel for the school's use only—it helps with figuring expenses for taxes.

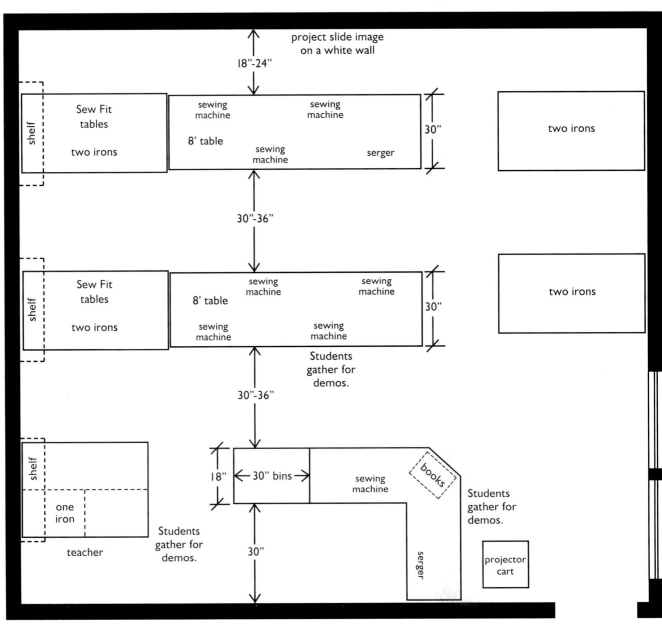

Adult Classroom
18' x 16.5'

Teaching Children

Winky Cherry has been teaching children to sew for over 20 years and has developed a successful in-depth program including a series of books and a teacher's manual and video (see Palmer/Pletsch Products).

Hundreds of children have spent many happy hours in Winky's single-car garage converted into a sewing school. She has equipped the school with four Singer Featherweight machines in cabinets and one serger. A lot of her program is hand sewing so she has two banquet tables for the children to gather around. She cut the table legs down to make the height appropriate for the young child. Many times children make projects as gifts, so Winky has a gift-wrap bin in the classroom. She installed a large bulletin board to display ideas and completed projects. Shelves line two walls of the classroom and store needed supplies and fabric. One shelf system was designed with slide-out bins.

To create this system, she screwed wood strips to the vertical support panels. These strips act as runners for plastic wash bins. To give a finished look to the room, Winky covered the shelf system with a fabric curtain hung on a tension rod.

Winky Cherry

An activity table large enough to seat six children plus the teacher can be purchased from a school supply store. It is perfect for teaching children. You can easily see, reach and help all children from one location, and it's sized for children!

22-30"   72"

Children's Classroom

Winky Cherry converted a single car garage into a sewing school. She built shelf systems to line two walls and invested in 6' banquet tables, chairs and four machines.

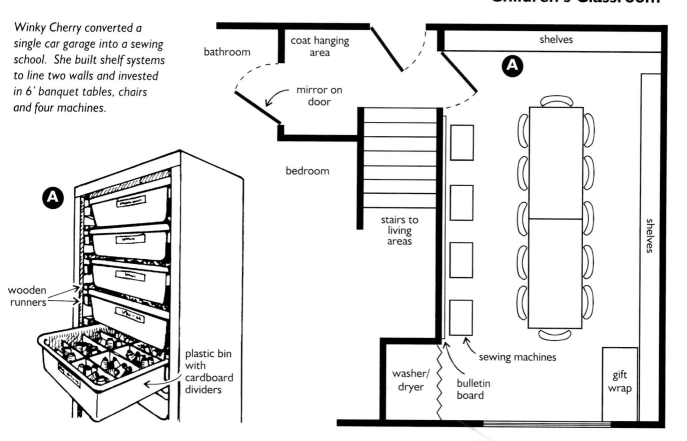

wooden runners

plastic bin with cardboard dividers

bathroom

coat hanging area

mirror on door

bedroom

stairs to living areas

washer/ dryer

bulletin board

sewing machines

shelves

shelves

gift wrap

OH! THOSE CLOSETS

For many of us, finding storage space for our sewing paraphanalia is our biggest challenge. It's logical to use the closets in our home, but they are already stuffed full! Closet organization may be the key for carving out more storage space. A wide array of closet storage units and accessories can be found in builders supply, housewares and specialty stores.

CLOTHING INVENTORY

Identify your needs and the spatial requirements of clothing and household goods before planning the closet. Here is a checklist, followed by dimensional information on typical clothing and linen storage.

WOMEN

Height _____

Reach _____

Ceiling Height _____

Hanging Space Requirements

_____ Shirts _____ Length

_____ Skirts _____ Length

_____ Pants _____ Length

_____ Jackets _____ Length

_____ Coats _____ Length

_____ Dresses _____ Length

_____ Jumpsuits _____ Length

_____ Evening Dresses _____ Length

_____ Robes _____ Length

_____ Other _____ Length

_____ Other _____ Length

Miscellaneous Storage

_____ Belts

_____ Scarves

_____ Necklaces

_____ Other Jewelry

Related Storage

Soiled Clothing Hamper Size _____

Mirror Size _____

Travel Rod/Temporary Hanging Size _____

Suitcase Storage _____

Packing Shelf _____

    Size _____"x _____"x _____"

    Size _____"x _____"x _____"

Iron/Ironing Board _____

Briefcase Shelf _____

Sitting Area _____

Other _____

Other _____

Shelf or Drawer Space Requirements

_____ Sweaters _____ Folded Size

_____ T-Shirts _____ Folded Size

_____ Shorts _____ Folded Size

_____ Swimsuits _____ Folded Size

_____ Beach Cover-ups _____ Folded

_____ Full Slips _____ Folded

_____ Half Slips _____ Folded Size

_____ Camisoles _____ Folded Size

_____ Bras _____ Folded Size

_____ Underwear _____ Folded Size

_____ Nylons/Pantyhose _____ Folded

_____ Socks _____ Folded

    _____ Rolled

_____ Nightgowns/Pajamas __ Folded

_____ Shoes _____ Inches

_____ Maintained in Boxes? _____

_____ Purses

_____ Hats

_____ Gloves

_____ Handkerchiefs

_____ Other

_____ Other

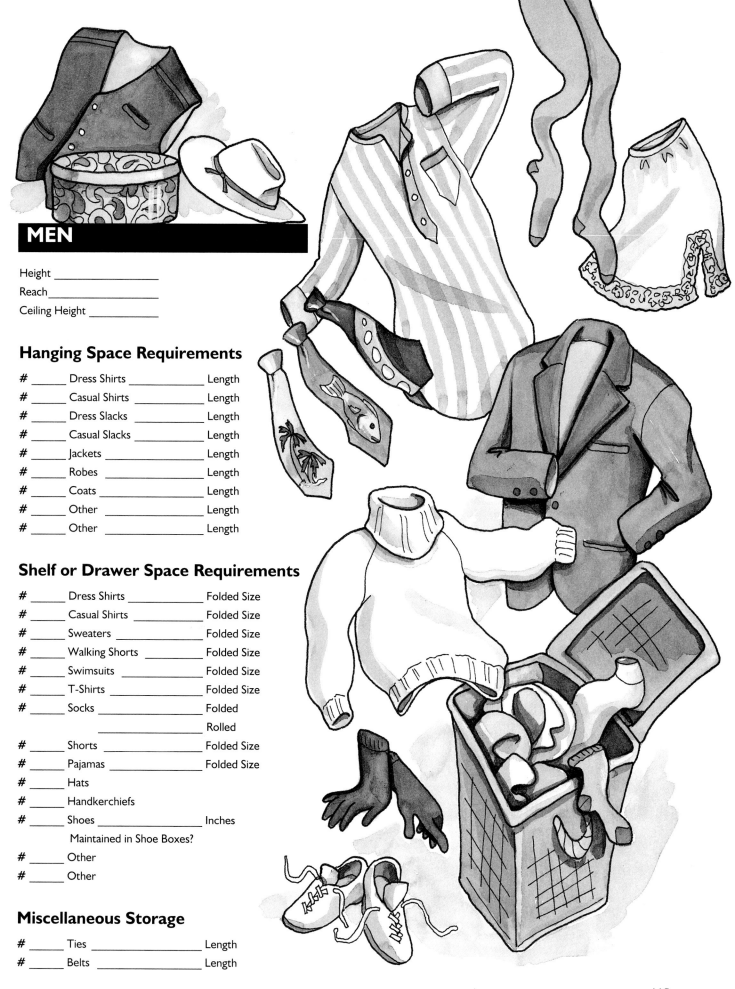

MEN

Height _____

Reach_____

Ceiling Height _____

Hanging Space Requirements

# _____	Dress Shirts _____	Length
# _____	Casual Shirts _____	Length
# _____	Dress Slacks _____	Length
# _____	Casual Slacks _____	Length
# _____	Jackets _____	Length
# _____	Robes _____	Length
# _____	Coats _____	Length
# _____	Other _____	Length
# _____	Other _____	Length

Shelf or Drawer Space Requirements

# _____	Dress Shirts _____	Folded Size
# _____	Casual Shirts _____	Folded Size
# _____	Sweaters _____	Folded Size
# _____	Walking Shorts _____	Folded Size
# _____	Swimsuits _____	Folded Size
# _____	T-Shirts _____	Folded Size
# _____	Socks _____	Folded
	_____	Rolled
# _____	Shorts _____	Folded Size
# _____	Pajamas _____	Folded Size
# _____	Hats	
# _____	Handkerchiefs	
# _____	Shoes _____	Inches
	Maintained in Shoe Boxes?	
# _____	Other	
# _____	Other	

Miscellaneous Storage

# _____	Ties _____	Length
# _____	Belts _____	Length

Typical Dimensions—Women's Clothing & Accesories

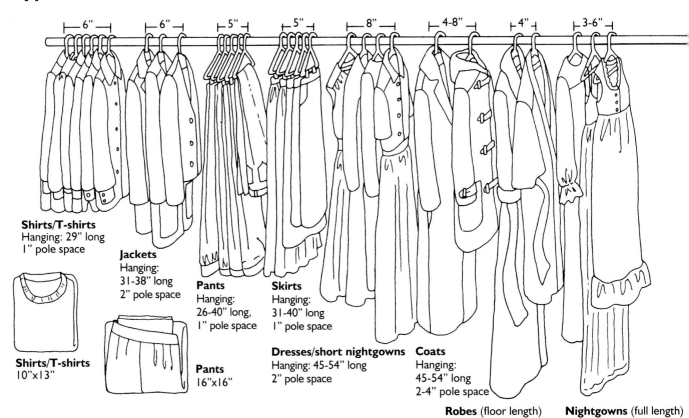

Shirts/T-shirts
Hanging: 29" long
1" pole space

Shirts/T-shirts
10"x13"

Jackets
Hanging:
31-38" long
2" pole space

Pants
Hanging:
26-40" long,
1" pole space

Pants
16"x16"

Skirts
Hanging:
31-40" long
1" pole space

Dresses/short nightgowns
Hanging: 45-54" long
2" pole space

Coats
Hanging:
45-54" long
2-4" pole space

Robes (floor length)
Hanging: 60-64" long
2" pole space

Nightgowns (full length)
Hanging: 60-64" long
1-2" pole space

Men's Clothing & Accessories

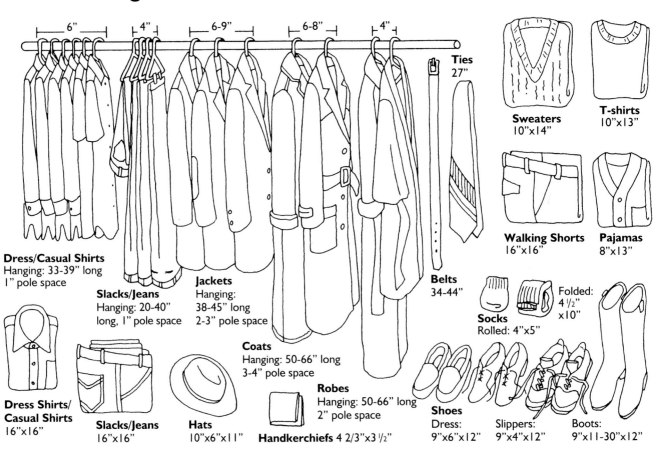

Dress/Casual Shirts
Hanging: 33-39" long
1" pole space

**Dress Shirts/
Casual Shirts**
16"x16"

Slacks/Jeans
Hanging: 20-40"
long, 1" pole space

Slacks/Jeans
16"x16"

Jackets
Hanging:
38-45" long
2-3" pole space

Coats
Hanging: 50-66" long
3-4" pole space

Hats
10"x6"x11"

Robes
Hanging: 50-66" long
2" pole space

Handkerchiefs 4 2/3"x3 1/2"

Ties
27"

Belts
34-44"

Sweaters
10"x14"

T-shirts
10"x13"

Walking Shorts
16"x16"

Pajamas
8"x13"

Socks
Rolled: 4"x5"

Folded:
4 1/2"
x10"

Shoes
Dress:
9"x6"x12"

Slippers:
9"x4"x12"

Boots:
9"x11-30"x12"

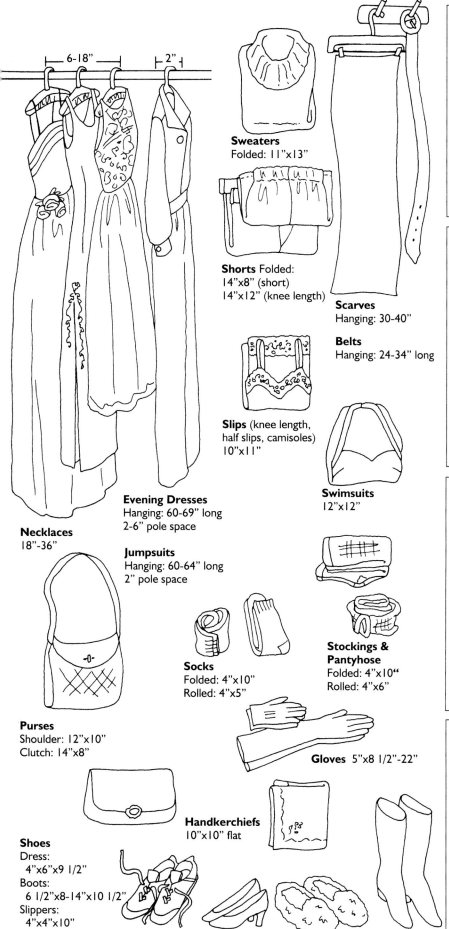

6-18" | **2"**

Sweaters
Folded: 11"x13"

Shorts Folded:
14"x8" (short)
14"x12" (knee length)

Scarves
Hanging: 30-40"

Belts
Hanging: 24-34" long

Slips (knee length,
half slips, camisoles)
10"x11"

Swimsuits
12"x12"

Evening Dresses
Hanging: 60-69" long
2-6" pole space

Necklaces
18"-36"

Jumpsuits
Hanging: 60-64" long
2" pole space

**Stockings &
Pantyhose**
Folded: 4"x10"
Rolled: 4"x6"

Socks
Folded: 4"x10"
Rolled: 4"x5"

Purses
Shoulder: 12"x10"
Clutch: 14"x8"

Gloves 5"x8 1/2"-22"

Handkerchiefs
10"x10" flat

Shoes
Dress:
4"x6"x9 1/2"
Boots:
6 1/2"x8-14"x10 1/2"
Slippers:
4"x4"x10"

Typical Closet Accessory Dimensions

Built-in Shoe Racks: 9"x6" each cubby
Free-standing Floor Shoe Rack: 21"x8"x10"
Shoe Bag: 20"x36"x8"
                      13"x57"x15"
Purse Rack: no. of purses x12"x10"
Hat Box: 12" and 14" diameter
Garment Bag: 20"-21" x 57"x 8"-24"
Boot Rack: 18"
Tie Rack: 18"
Hangers: 16-21"

Recommended Rod Placement and Support

Rod heights (height of rod and shelf above rod) may vary according to the height and vertical reach of the person using the closet and the length of clothing owned. Common rod heights for clothes are as follows:

Item	Height from Floor
Floor-length Gowns/Robes	68-72"
Street-length Dresses/Coats	54-63"
Shirts/Pants/Skirts/Jackets	48"
Children's Clothing	32-45"
Double Pole (apart)	36-45"

Recommended Maximum Span

Pole Size	Max. Span
Wood 1 1/8" diameter	3 feet
Wood 1 3/8" diameter	4 feet
Wood 1 5/8" diameter	5 feet
Metal 3/4" diameter	6 feet
Metal 1" diameter	8 feet
Metal 1 1/4" diameter	10 feet

Shelves should be 2-3" above rods to allow space to lift the hanger off the rod without hitting the overhead surface.

Recommended Maximum Loads for Shelving

	Plywood Thickness			
Span	3/8"	1/2"	5/8"	3/4"
12"	163	330	593	817
16"	68	138	249	374
20"	35	71	127	191
24"	20	41	75	111
32"	-	17	30	46
36"	-	12	22	33
40"	-	-	16	24
48"	-	-	10	14

(Maximum load: pounds per square feet)

MINIMUM CLOSET SIZES

Reach-in Closet

The minimum front-to-back depth of space for hanging clothes is 24". The accessible rod length is equal to the width of the door opening, plus 6" on each side.

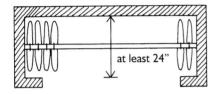

at least 24"

Edge-in Closet

With an edge-in space of at least 18", the accessible rod length can be much longer than the door width.

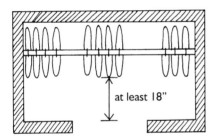

at least 18"

Walk-in Closet

This type provides rods on one, two or three sides of an access path at least 20" wide. A wider access space within the closet may be used as a dressing area.

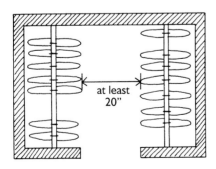

at least 20"

CLOSET SOLUTIONS

Now that you know what you have to store and how much space is needed, what do you do now? How can you rearrange the space or organize the closet better to free up space? Let's look at some "before" and "after" closets to give you ideas.

Reorganize a Walk-In Closet

Create an empty closet to claim for sewing by reorganizing and redesigning two closets...

HIS   **HERS**

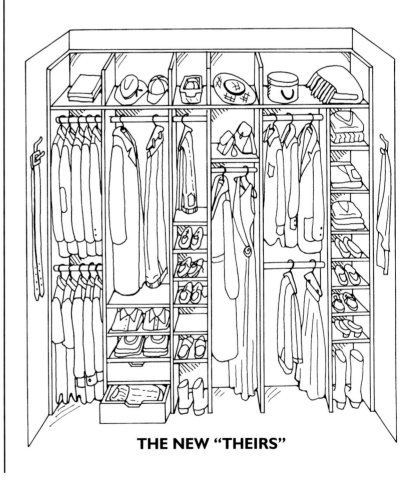

THE NEW "THEIRS"

Reorganize a Walk-In Closet

Using just two walls of this walk-in closet for clothing really opened up the space, and actually provides more storage (no "lost" corner spaces). Double poling, dresser drawers and high shelves all add usable space.

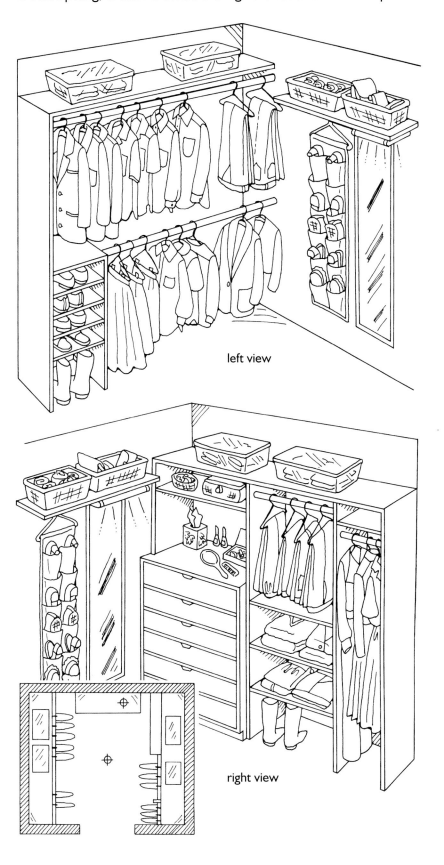

left view

right view

A Coat Closet Reorganization

A coat closet doesn't have to be a jumble. Consider dropping the pole height down for the longest coat and adding more shelves above for hats and gloves. A simple shoe rack keeps books and shoes organized.

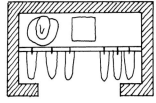

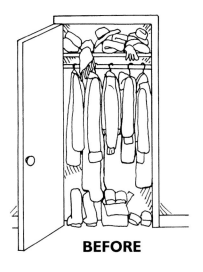

BEFORE

THE LINEN CLOSET

Another closet that may benefit from re-organization is the linen closet. Are linens scattered in more than one closet? Could they be combined into one if you customized your closet? Here's a possible solution:

Linen Dimensions

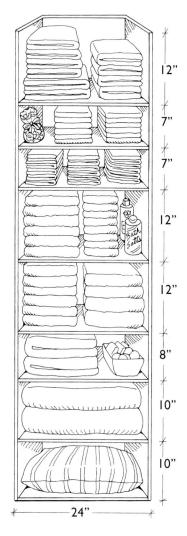

FLAT SHEETS:
Twin
72"x108" fold to 9"x13 1/2"
Double
81"x108" fold to 10 1/8"x13 1/2"
Queen
90"x115" fold to 11 1/4x14 3/8"
King
108"x120" fold to 13 1/2"x 15"

FITTED SHEETS:
Twin
39"x76" fold to 9 3/4"x 9 1/2"
Double
54"x76" fold to 13 1/2"x9 1/2"
Queen
60"x80" fold to 15"x10"
King
72"x84" fold to 18"x10 1/2"

Standard Pillowcases
21"x33" fold to 7"x11"
King Pillowcases
21"x45" fold to 7"x15"

Twin Blanket
66"x90" fold to 16 1/2" x 22 1/2"
72"x90" fold to 18"x22 1/2"
Double Blanket
80"x90" fold to 20"x22 1/2"
Queen/King Blanket
108"x90" fold to 27"x 22 1/2"

Hand Towel
11"x18" fold to 5 1/2"x9"
12"x20" fold to 6"x10"

Face Towel
15"x26" fold to 7 1/2"x 13"
16"x32" fold to 8"x16"
18"x36" fold to 9"x18"

Bath Towel
22"x44" fold to 11"x 11"
24"x48" fold to 12"x 12"
26"x50" fold to 13"x 12 1/2"
28"x52" fold to 14"x 13"

Bath Sheet
36"x68" fold to 12"x17"
44"x72" fold to 14 3/4"x18"

Wash Cloth
9"x9" fold to 4 1/2" x 9"
12"x12" fold to 6"x12"
14"x14" fold to 7"x14"

Bath Mat
20"x30" fold to 10"x 7 1/2"
20"x34" fold to 10"x 8 1/2"
22"x36" fold to 10"x 9"

Note: There is no standard method of folding linens. Fold to fit your storage area.

THE FOOD PANTRY

The best shelf depth for storage of cans, jars and food boxes is 9". Storage of extra pots, pans, bowls, etc., should be 12". Vary the shelf depths as needed so you can store as much as possible in as little space as possible. By reorganizing my food pantry (I changed the depth and height of the shelves for specialized needs) I opened up space for sewing storage adjacent to my sewing/office area (see page 93).

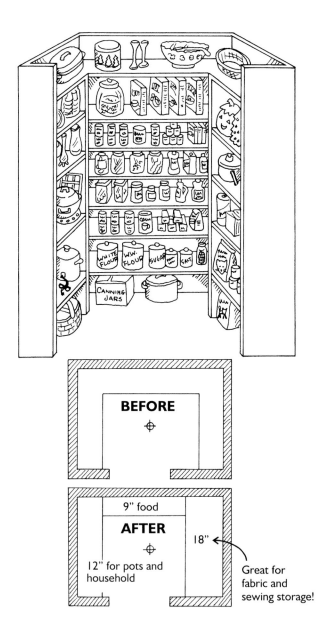

If space allows, consider creating bays (as shown on page 104) to use for food storage. Think of your pantry as an efficient grocery store!

THE MURPHY BED & CUT/PRESS TABLE

The Murphy Bed

This is a simple design for the Murphy bed on pages 88 & 89.

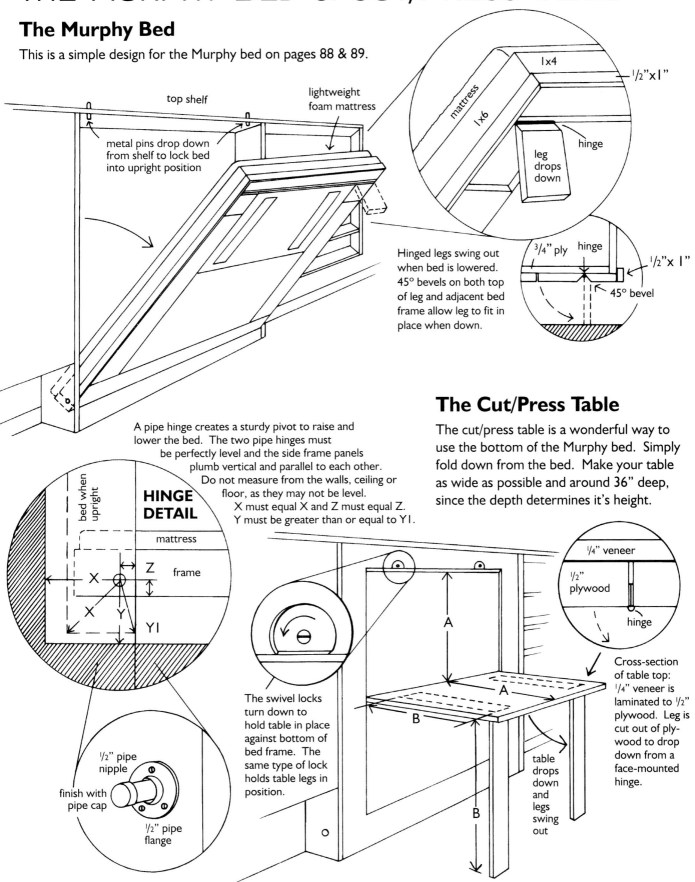

top shelf

lightweight foam mattress

metal pins drop down from shelf to lock bed into upright position

mattress 1x6 1x4 ¹/₂"x1" hinge leg drops down

Hinged legs swing out when bed is lowered. 45° bevels on both top of leg and adjacent bed frame allow leg to fit in place when down.

³/₄" ply hinge ¹/₂"x 1" 45° bevel

A pipe hinge creates a sturdy pivot to raise and lower the bed. The two pipe hinges must be perfectly level and the side frame panels plumb vertical and parallel to each other. Do not measure from the walls, ceiling or floor, as they may not be level. X must equal X and Z must equal Z. Y must be greater than or equal to Y1.

bed when upright

HINGE DETAIL

mattress
frame
X Z X Y Y1

¹/₂" pipe nipple
finish with pipe cap
¹/₂" pipe flange

The Cut/Press Table

The cut/press table is a wonderful way to use the bottom of the Murphy bed. Simply fold down from the bed. Make your table as wide as possible and around 36" deep, since the depth determines it's height.

The swivel locks turn down to hold table in place against bottom of bed frame. The same type of lock holds table legs in position.

¹/₄" veneer
¹/₂" plywood
hinge

Cross-section of table top: ¹/₄" veneer is laminated to ¹/₂" plywood. Leg is cut out of plywood to drop down from a face-mounted hinge.

table drops down and legs swing out

A A B B

RESOURCES

Cabinets, Chairs, Cutting Tables

Create-A-Space
P.O. Box 4793
Oak Brook, IL 60522-4793
708/654-8671

Horn of America
2128 North US Highway 1
Ft. Pierce, FL 34946
-OR-
P.O. Box 608
Sutton, West Virginia 26601
800/882-8845

Parsons Cabinet, Inc.
420 W. Parsons Dr.
P.O. Box 445
Osceola, AR 72370
800/643-0090
501/563-6360 fax

Ritter Cabinet Manufacturing
Mottman Industrial Park
2948 29th St. SW
Tumwater, WA 98512
800/736-7374 • 206/352-0753 fax

Roberts Manufacturing
120 W. 300 S.
American Fork, UT 84003
800/658-8795 • 801/756-5758 fax

Sewing Center Supply
9631 NE Colfax
Portland, OR 97220
503/252-1452

Sirco Tables
Box 2463
Missoula, MT 59806
800/621-3792 • 800/445-5281 fax

Sew/Fit Co.
P.O. Box 397
Bedford Park, IL 60499
800/547-4739
708/458-5665 fax

Tacony Corporation
1760 Gilsinne Lane
Fenton, MO 63026
314/349-3000

Voster Marketing
190 Mt. Pleasant Rd.
Newtown, CT 06470
203/270-7190

Cabinet Lifts

Maryland Sewing Machine Center
6280 Branch Ave.
Camp Springs, MD 20748
301/899-7200

Calloni Italy
Via Paganini
8-20030 Barlassina
Milano Italy
011/392-560558

Mail Order Catalogs

A Great Notion
5630 Landmark Way, Unit 101
Surrey, BC, Canada U35 7H1
604/533-2891
604/533-7563 fax

Brookstone, Hard to Find Tools
17 Riverside St.
Nashua, NH 03062
800/926-7000

Clotilde
2 Sew Smart Way
P.O. Box 88031
Stevens Point, WI 54481-8031
800/772-2891
715/341-3082 fax

Golden Ventures, Inc.
   Homecare Products
Box 90230
Indianapolis, IN 46290-0230
800/578-4663

Hold Everything
P.O. Box 7807
San Francisco, CA 94120-7807
800/1421-2264

Lillian Vernon
Virginia Beach, VA 23479-0002
804/430-1500
804/430-1010 fax

Nancy's Notions
P.O. Box 683
Beaver Dam, WI 53916
800/833-0690
800/255-8119 fax

Plow & Hearth
P.O. Box 5000
Madison, VI 22727-1500
800/627-1712

Renovator's
P.O. Box 2515
Conway, NH 03818-2515
800/659-2211
603/447-1717 fax

S & B Notions
#512-381 Bayview Ave
N. York, ONT
Canada M2K 2Y2
416/226-1966
416/226-2040 fax

The Woodworker's Store
21801 Industrial Blvd.
Rogers, MN 55374-9514
800/279-4441
612/428-8668 fax

Woodcraft
210 Wood County Industrial Park
P.O. Box 1686
Parksburg, WV 26102-1686
800/535-4482

Thread Racks, Notion Organizers

Blue Feather Products
2895 Hwy 66
Ashland, OR 97520
800/472-2487 • 503/482-2338
503/482-2338 fax

Carter's Workshop
RR2, Box 251
Rogers, AR 72756
800/776-1699

Coats and Clark
P.O. Box 27067
Greenville, SC 29616
803/234-0331

Creative Carriers
1311 Fort Street
Buffalo, WY 82834
800/848-5684

Dartek Company Supply
949 Larch Ave.
Elmhurst, IL 60126
800/832-7835

Eagle Affiliates
Harrison, NJ 07029
800/643-6798
201/481-6772 fax

Fabriholic's Treasure Chest
Sew Sensational
Joan Stoicheff
7345 N. Lesley Ave.
Indianapolis, IN 46250
317/842-9662

Frostline Kits
2525 River Road
Grand Junction, CO 81505
800/548-7872
970/243-8553 fax

M&M Custom Woodshop
P.O. Box 296
39843 Mt. Hope Dr.
Lebanon, OR 97355
503/258-3078

Rubbermaid
Wooster, OH 44691
216/264-6464 ext. 2619

The Sewing Rack
by Dezzie's Incorporated
P.O. Box 6737
Fort Worth, TX 76115-6737
800/858-1653

June Tailor, Inc.
P.O. Box 208
Richfield, WI 53076
800/844-5400
800/246-1573 fax

Wall Systems

Grand & Benedicts, Inc.
401 NE Second Ave.
Portland, OR 97232
800/547-7005
503/232-6519 fax

Rindler Display
Seattle Trade Center
2601 Elliott Ave., Rm 1306
Seattle, WA 98121
206/441-3145
206/728-5853 fax

Schulte Corporation
Cincinnati, OH 45249
513/489-9300
513/247-3389 fax

Wesystems
D.L. West Manufacturing
4956 West 119th Place
Hawthorne, CA 90250-2723
310/675-6733 • 310/679-2688 fax

MISC.

Joanne DiBenedetto Burdick
DiBenedetto Design
Pacific Design Cabinetry
6050 SE Alexander
Hillsboro, OR 97123
503/848-8010 • 503/848-9462 fax

Sewing Room Posters
Ghee's
2620 Centenary Blvd. #3-205
Shreveport, LA 71104
318/226-1701

Instant Interiors
P.O. Box 1793
Eugene, OR 97440
541/689-4608

Labours of Love
Debra Justice
3760 Old Clayburn Road
Abbotsford, BC, Canada V3G 1H8
604/853-9132

Mamma Ro'
P.O. Box 12046
Portland, OR 97212-0046
800/728-3784

Mary Mulari
Mary's Productions
217 N. Main
Box 87
Aurora, MN 55705
218/229-2804 • 218/229-2533 fax

Jo Reimer, fiber artist
Travel Vest Pattern
11990 NW Maple Hill Lane
Portland, OR 97229-4720
503/643-1968 • 503/643-0764 fax

Kelley Salber, artist
Clocks and Custom Collage
335 SE 29th
Portland, OR 97214
503/230-0256

BIBLIOGRAPHY

Books

**Beyond the Basics
  Advanced Kitchen Design**
Ellen Cheever, CKD, CBD, ASID
Sponsored by
National Kitchen and Bath Association
Hackettstown, NJ 07840

Home Offices and Workspaces
Sunset Books
Lane Publishing Co.
Menlo Park, CA 94025

**Sitting on the Job, How to Survive the
  Stresses of Sitting Down to Work**
Scott W. Donkin, DC
Houghton Miffin Company
2 Park St.
Boston, MA 02108

Magazines

Sew News Magazine
P.O. Box 1790
Peoria, IL 61656-1790

Threads Magazine
The Taunton Press
Box 355
Newtown, CT 06470

Kitchen and Bath Business
P.O. Box 469051
Escondido, CA 92046-9051

NOTES

INDEX

Palmer/Pletsch PRODUCTS

These ready-to-use, information-filled sewing how-to books, manuals and videos can be found in local fabric stores or ordered through Palmer/Pletsch Publishing (see address on last page).

8¹/₂x11 BOOKS

☐ **The BUSINE$$ of Teaching Sewing,** *by Marcy Miller and Pati Palmer, 128 pages, $19.95* If you want to be in the BUSINESS of teaching sewing, read this book which compiles 20 years of experience of Palmer/Pletsch, plus Miller's innovative ideas. Chapters include: Appearance and Image; Getting Started; The Lesson Plan; Class Formats; Location; Marketing, Promotion & Advertising; Pricing; Teaching Techniques; and Continuing Education—Where To Find It.

☐ **Couture—The Art of Fine Sewing**, *by Roberta C. Carr, 208 pages, softcover, $29.95* How-to's of couture techniques and secrets, brought to life with illustrations and dozens of garments photographed in full color.

☐ **The Serger Idea Book—A Collection of Inspiring Ideas from Palmer/Pletsch,** *160 pgs., $19.95* Color photos and how-to's on inspiring and fashionable ideas from the Extraordinary to the Practical.

☐ **Creative Serging for the Home— And Other Quick Decorating Ideas,** *by Lynette Ranney Black and Linda Wisner, 160 pgs., $18.95* Color photos and how-to's to help you transform your home into the place YOU want it to be.

☐ **Sewing Ultrasuede® Brand Fabrics—Ultrasuede®, Ultrasuede Light™, Caress™, Ultraleather™,** *by Marta Alto, Pati Palmer and Barbara Weiland, 128 pages, $16.95* Color photo section, plus the newest techniques to master these luxurious fabrics.

☐ **Dream Sewing Spaces—Design and Organization for Spaces Large and Small,** *by Lynette Ranney Black, 128 pages, $19.95* Make your dream a reality. Analyze your needs and your space, then learn to plan and put it together. Lots of color photos!

Coming in early 1996:
☐ **The Palmer/Pletsch FIT Book** *by Marta Alto & Pati Palmer.* The authors write from 25 years of hands-on experience fitting thousands of people. Their practical approach is explained in their simple, logical style. Learn to finally buy the right size, then tissue fit to determine alterations. Special sections include fitting young teen girls, history of sizing, and fitting REAL people. Write or call for publication date and more information.

5¹/₂x8¹/₂ BOOKS

☐ **Sew to Success!—How to Make Money in a Home-Based Sewing Business,** *by Kathleen Spike, 128 pgs., $10.95* Learn how to establish your market, set policies and procedures, price your talents and more!

☐ **Mother Pletsch's Painless Sewing**, *NEW Revised Edition, by Pati Palmer and Susan Pletsch, 128 pgs., $8.95* The most uncomplicated sewing book of the century! Filled with sewing tips on how to sew FAST!

Book are also available in spiralbound— 3.00 additional for large books, $2.00 for all.

126

☐ **Sewing With Sergers—The Complete Handbook for Overlock Sewing,** *Revised Edition, by Pati Palmer and Gail Brown, 128 pages, $8.95* Learn easy threading tips, stitch types, rolled edging and flat-locking on your serger.

☐ **Creative Serging—The Complete Handbook for Decorative Overlock Sewing,** *by Pati Palmer, Gail Brown and Sue Green, 128 pages, $8.95* In-depth information and creative uses of your serger.

☐ **Sensational Silk—A Handbook for Sewing Silk and Silk-like Fabrics,** *by Gail Brown, 128 pgs., $6.95* Complete guide for sewing with silk and silkies, plus all kinds of great blouse and dress techniques.

☐ **Pants For Any Body,** *Revised Edition, by Pati Palmer and Susan Pletsch, 128 pgs., $8.95* Learn to fit pants with clear step-by-step problem and solution illustrations.

☐ **Easy, Easier, Easiest Tailoring,** *Revised Edition, by Pati Palmer and Susan Pletsch, 128 pgs., $8.95* Learn 4 different tailoring methods, easy fit tips, and timesaving machine lining.

☐ **Clothes Sense—Straight Talk About Wardrobe Planning,** *by Barbara Weiland and Leslie Wood, 128 pgs., $6.95* Learn to define your personal style and when to sew or buy.

☐ **Sew a Beautiful Wedding,** *by Gail Brown and Karen Dillon, 128 pgs., $8.95* Bridal how-to's from choosing the most flattering style to sewing with specialty fabrics.

☐ **Decorating with Fabric: An Idea Book,** *by Judy Lindahl, 128 pgs., $6.95* Learn to cover walls, create canopies, valances, pillows, lamp shades, and more!

☐ **The Shade Book,** *Revised Edition, by Judy Lindahl, 152 pages, $9.95* Learn six major shade types, variations, trimmings, hardware, hemming, care, and upkeep.

☐ **Original Roo (The Purple Kangaroo),** *by Bob Benz, 48 pages, $5.95* A whimsical children's story about a kangaroo's adventures and how she saves the day with sewing.

Level III
Level I
Level II
Level IV

MY FIRST SEWING BOOK KITS

My First Sewing Books are packaged as kits, complete with materials for a first project. These kits, along with the Teaching Manual & Video offer a complete and thoroughly tested sewing program for young children. 5-to-11-year olds learn patience, manners, creativity, completion and how to follow rules...all through the enjoyment of sewing. Each book follows a project from start to finish with clever rhymes and clear illustrations. *Each book, 8 1/2" x 8 1/2", 40 pgs., $12.95*

☐ **My First Sewing Book,** *by Winky Cherry.* Children as young as 5 hand sew and stuff a felt bird shape. Also available in Spanish.

☐ **My First Embroidery Book,** *by Winky Cherry.* Beginners learn the importance of accuracy by making straight stitches, including the running and satin stitch, using a chart and gingham squares to make a name sampler.

☐ **My First Doll Book,** *by Winky Cherry.* These felt dolls have embroidered faces, yarn hair, and clothes. Children use the overstitch and embroidery skills learned in levels I and II.

☐ **My First Machine Sewing Book,** *by Winky Cherry.* With practice pages, then a fabric star, children learn about machine parts, seam allowances, tapering, snips, clips, stitching wrong sides out, and turning a shape right side out.

☐ **Teaching Children to Sew Manual and Video,** *$39.95*
The 112-page, 8 1/2"x 11" **Teaching Manual**, tells you exactly how to teach young children, including preparing the environment, workshop space, class control, and the importance of incorporating other life skills along with sewing skills. In the **Video**, see Winky Cherry teach six 6-to-8 year olds how to sew in a true-life classroom setting. Watch how she introduces herself and explains the rules and shows them how to sew. Then, see close-ups of a child sewing the project in double-time. This part could be shown to your students. Finally, Winky gives you a tour of an ideal classroom setup. She also talks about the tools, patterns and sewing supplies you will need.
1 hour.

☐ **Teacher's Starter Kit,** *$49.95*
The refillable kit includes these hard-to-find items—a retail value of $73.00: 50 felt pieces in assorted colors (9 x 12"), 6 colors of crochet thread on balls, 2 packs of needles with large eyes, 2 pin cushions, 12 pre-cut birds, and printed patterns for shapes.

Deluxe Kits and additional class-room materials are available. Ask for our "As Easy As ABC" catalog.

VIDEOS

According to Robbie Fanning, author and critic, "The most professional of all the (video) tapes we've seen is Pati Palmer's *Sewing Today the Time Saving Way.* This tape should serve as the standard of excellence in the field." Following that standard, we have produced 8 more videos since Time Saving! *Videos are $29.95 each.*

☐ **Sewing Today the Time Saving Way,** 45 minutes featuring Lynn Raasch & Karen Dillon sharing tips and techniques to make sewing fun, fast and trouble free.

☐ **Sewing to Success!,** 45 minutes featuring Kathleen Spike who presents a wealth of information on how to achieve financial freedom working in your home as a professional dressmaker.

☐ **Sewing With Sergers—Basics,** 1 hour featuring Marta Alto & Pati Palmer on tensions, stitch types and their uses, serging circles, turning corners, gathering and much more.

☐ **Sewing With Sergers—Advanced,** 1 hour featuring Marta Alto & Pati Palmer on in-depth how-to's for rolled edging & flatlocking as well as garment details.

☐ **Creative Serging,** 1 hour featuring Marta Alto & Pati Palmer on how to use decorative threads, yarns and ribbons on your serger. PLUS: fashion shots!

☐ **Creative Serging II,** 1 hour featuring Marta Alto & Pati Palmer showing more creative ideas, including in-depth creative rolled edge.

☐ **Two-Hour Trousers,** 1 hour, 40 minutes, featuring Kathleen Spike with fit tips using our unique tissue fitting techniques, the best basics, and designer details.

☐ **Sewing Ultrasuede® Brand Fabrics— Ultrasuede®, Facile®, Caress™, Ultra-leather™** 1 hour featuring Marta Alto and Pati Palmer with clear, step-by-step sewing demonstrations and fashion show.

☐ **Creative Home Decorating Ideas: Sewing Projects for the Home,** 1 hour featuring Lynette Ranney Black showing creative, easy ideas for windows, walls, tables and more. Companion to *Creative Serging for the Home.*

*An additional video from Palmer/Pletsch is available on **Teaching Children to Sew**, as part of a training package described on the previous page.*

TRENDS BULLETINS

Trends Bulletins are comprehensive 8-12 page two-color publications designed to keep you up-to-date by bringing you the best and the newest information on your favorite sewing topics.

☐ **Knitting Machines—An Introduction,** *by Terri Burns,* presents the basics of machine knitting, including stitch patterns, explanation of single and double bed machines, and a step-by-step guide to making your purchasing decision. *$3.95*

PALMER/PLETSCH WORKSHOPS

Our "Sewing Vacations" are offered on a variety of topics, including *Pant Fit, Fit, Tailoring, Creative Serging, Ultrasuede,* and a special *Best of Palmer/Pletsch* session. Workshops are held at the new Palmer/Pletsch International Training Center near the Portland, Oregon, airport. **Teacher training** sessions are also available on each topic. They include practice teaching sessions, hair styling, make-up and publicity photo session, up to 300 slides and script, camera-ready workbook handouts and publicity flyer and the manual **The BUSINE$$ of Teaching Sewing.** Call or write for schedules and information:

Lynette Ranney Black, coordinator
1629 S. Eaden Road
Oregon City, OR 97045
(503) 631-7443

Palmer/Pletsch also carries hard-to-find and unique notions including Perfect Sew Wash-Away Fabric Stabilizer, Perfect Sew Needle Threader and decorative serging threads. Check your local fabric store or contact Palmer/Pletsch Publishing, P.O. Box 12046, Portland, OR 97212-0046. (503) 274-0687 or 1-800-728-3784 (order desk).